the
CHILDREN
of NOW

the CHILDREN of NOW

Crystalline Children, Indigo Children,
Star Kids, Angels on Earth,
and the Phenomenon of Transitional Children

MEG BLACKBURN LOSEY, Msc.D., Ph.D.

NEW PAGE BOOKS
A division of The Career Press, Inc.
Pompton Plains, NJ

THE CHILDREN OF NOW
EDITED BY KIRSTEN DALLEY
TYPESET BY ASTRID deRIDDER
Cover design by Scott Fray
Printed in the U.S.A.

To order this title, please call toll-free 1-800-CAREER-1 (NJ and Canada: 201-848-0310) to order using VISA or MasterCard, or for further information on books from Career Press.

The Career Press, Inc., 220 West Parkway, Unit 12
Pompton Plains, NJ 07444
www.careerpress.com
www.newpagebooks.com

Library of Congress Cataloging-in-Publication Data

Losey, Meg Blackburn.
    The children of now : crystalline children, indigo children, star kids, angels on earth, and the phenomenon of transitional children / by Meg Blackburn Losey.
        p. cm.
    Includes bibliographical references and index.
    ISBN-13: 978-1-56414-948-0
    ISBN-10: 1-56414-948-X
    1. Children--psychic ability. 2. Children--Miscellanea. 3. Parapsychology. I. Title.

BF1045.C45L67 2006
133.8083—dc22

                                        200603487

DISCLAIMER

The author believes that many of the characteristics exhibited by the special children described in this book may best be explained and understood through her theories and paradigms. However, because not all symptoms or manifestations can be explained by the same cause, neither the author nor the publisher is in any way advising anyone to follow *or* reject any kind of treatment, medical or otherwise, in this book. Parents and guardians are urged to obtain as much information as possible when making *any* decisions that may affect the health and overall well-being of their children, and it is always advisable to consult a health-care professional. NO WARRANTY, EXPRESS OR IMPLIED, IS DELIVERED BY THE AUTHOR OR PUBLISHER WITH RESPECT TO THE CONTENTS OF THIS WORK.

DEDICATION

for Haley, Josh, and Devyn, lights of my world,
and all of the children who bring their magic
into this now and our future.

And for my David.

ACKNOWLEDGMENTS

In preparation for this work, I counseled and interviewed families, children, teachers, caregivers, medical personnel, and others too many to name individually. Great numbers of people contributed their stories to me via e-mail and in person, going out of their way to make sure I heard what they had to offer. To attempt to name each of you would be a disservice, as surely I would miss some. I am grateful beyond words for your candid sharing, the contributions you have made to my own expertise, and the loving grace with which nearly all of you nurture the Children of Now. With all that I am, I thank you!

I am particularly grateful for each and every child who has come to me for help, some calling out from the ethers and ultimately connecting with me in this plane of reality. It is my ardent desire that this book helps you to have an easier life, with support from all directions and tremendous nurturing as you become our future. You tell it like it is, bringing your giftedness to those who can hear you and even to some who cannot. You are beautiful and I love each of you dearly. You are all priceless gems in the heart of my being. It is always a privilege, an honor, and a pleasure to work with you.

Special acknowledgment goes to my little bug, Haley, who came into this world in 1999 with her eyes wide open. You gently but firmly took everyone into your light with your visions of angels, telepathic conversations, command of energy and movement, ability to sense and compare the vibrations of crystals, and to see the truth within others—even when those around you didn't admit it themselves. It was the awareness that you created within your "Memaw" that brought this book to life. I love you so.

Also, my gratitude to my publicist, Maggie Jessup. Maggie, I love that you don't take no for an answer, and I love how you go about getting the creative "yes"! Thank you so much for your ongoing efforts to get this work out into the world.

And to my agents Bill Gladstone and Ming at Waterside Productions: Many thanks for your confidence in my writing, and especially for taking this book into the mainstream where it will help countless others.

To Michael Pye and Career Press, my publisher: Thank you for believing in this book and getting it out there. The results of this information reaching the world will ripple outward in ways we may never know. The time really is now!

And lastly, but certainly not the least: To my husband David, for recognizing that my mission in life is greater than the two of us. You thank me for helping "all those people" each and every time I go out into the world. The freedom of your acceptance is priceless. Thank you, my love.

CONTENTS

FOREWORD

Dear Fellow Friends,
As you read this eye-opening, heart-inspiring book, ask yourself the following question: "How can I bless, honor, and support the New Children in their God-given mission in life?"

This is the lasting question, as we as a society are waking up to increasing numbers of these children who require soulful guidance. This book will assist each one of you, in polite and subtle ways, so that you can honor and gently guide these New Children.

Who would have thought we need guidance when we come across so sure, with a deep inner knowing from our cosmic adventures? Although my cosmic adventures have taken me all the way from walking beside Jesus to Atlantis, here I am "all-knowing" and innocent at the same time.

You see, we the Crystalline and Star Children may appear all-capable, yet we require the world's capacity for deep listening to resolve in our purpose and best effect change.

In my own personal experience, when I feel deeply heard, I feel a relaxation in every cell of my body. This relaxation is most amazing to bring change. I have learned in my own life, living as a child of the universe, yet in a unique body with its own mind, that I feel the most supported with the relaxation that comes from deep listening.

So, give a big hand to our almighty God for our wide-eyed innocence and amazing gifts, as the world takes huge notice in turn. As the world pays attention on a grand scale, this book becomes a valuable tool to put us, the Crystalline Children, at much ease. Dr. Meg Blackburn Losey has the style, eloquence, and inspiring ability to bring this far-reaching message to all who can be served.

In the pages of this book, Dr. Meg Blackburn Losey offers thoughtful, well-counseled, and heart-warming advice on such provoking topics as school, nutrition, and environment that will nourish and sustain us. It will keep you reading as you learn how to support these soulful, centered, yet delicate creatures. Inherent within learning how to best support the new children, you are awakening on your own journey.

Now don't you see, we are not here for our own purpose, we are here for the universal purpose? This awakening is necessary, as we need a critical mass with pure love vibration to resonate with the Earth for its salvation. We, the New Children, are here to assist you in this movement.

Lastly, through this book, you will also come to know that the one unifying force for all matter is love. *Love is the voice of the New Children.* Deeply listen to all their messages and we are well on our way to blessing, honoring, and supporting them in their God-given mission in life.

Bringer of Light and Love,
Nicholas M. Tschense, 9 years

INTRODUCTION

I remember what it was like to be home.
It was a lot different than here. Everything was
beautiful. I loved everyone and they loved me back
equally. How come it doesn't feel like that here?
—Andrew, age 4

Who are the Children of Now? They are a new generation of children—undeniably evolved beyond previous generations—who come to our world with very special gifts. Many of them remember where they were before they came to Earth, often even remembering their past lives. The Children of Now fall into several distinct categories, and my research has shown that there are overlapping attributes that make it nearly impossible to pigeonhole these amazing beings into neat little boxes.

These children are *not* all Indigos! The Indigos are the paradigm busters, the ones who know inherently that there is something wrong in our world, and that society's rules do not always consider either the particular circumstances or the individuals in any given situation. By creating awareness, the Indigos have opened doors for us to recognize and nurture successive generations. There is already much information available about our wonderful Indigos in the form of books, articles, Websites, and movies.

This book focuses on children who are generally younger and who have evolved far beyond the Indigo Children. They are the Crystalline Children, the Star Kids, the Earth Angels, and the Transitional Children—the ones who fall in between. Each group exhibits amazing giftedness yet remains unique in its attributes. The Transitional Kids don't quite fit any of these categories, yet are every bit as special and amazing.

There isn't much information publicly available about the phenomena of these very different and remarkable children, except what has been spread by word of mouth. The reason for this is the same reason that most metaphysical subjects are not fully accepted by the general public. Purely energetic phenomena are hard to document and prove scientifically. Our technology does not yet have the capability to measure the subtle fields of energy or the very high frequency biophysical energy fields that our New Children carry. We all know, from a scientific or medical standpoint, that if something can't be quantified then it must not exist, right? Definitely not!

The study of metaphysics is just that—the study of everything outside of what science can measure. Regarding the children, there are too many coincidences to be ignored, too many seemingly unrelated families, caregivers, teachers, and children experiencing the same things across the globe for us to ignore this subject any longer.

This book is about what cannot yet be measured but happens every day in our world.

There are greater realities just beyond most people's perception. There are infinite dimensions within all of creation, and those dimensions are part of the construct of the One—that which is God, Spirit, or the Creator—and within all of these realities are infinite possibilities. To most of us, the idea of other realms, at least one that houses God, is very real. I am often awestruck by the fact that the general populace easily believes in a supreme being or a creator of all things, and yet cannot fathom the idea that they are an integral and vital part of that realm. We cannot believe that there are indeed worlds beyond this here and now, and that they affect us every moment we exist. In fact, for many, the idea of reality beyond the third dimension is frightening. It is my intention to stretch the reader's awareness of reality a little bit further, and to share realities beyond the scope of what we see, feel, hear, touch, smell, or sense—realities that have everything to do with us on infinite levels. It is from within these alternate realities that the Children of Now bring us what human beings have sought throughout our existence—namely, our God self.

We are created of layer after layer of subtle energy, and that energy communicates with all other levels of reality— inwardly, outwardly, and infinitely. The types of energy fields that are described herein are not supposition. My extrasensory giftedness carries me into multiple dimensions and beyond, where I can see, touch, taste, smell, and hear those layers.

Our physicality is just a small part of the vast reality, most of which we cannot access with our usual five senses, or even our intuitive nature (our "sixth sense"). When we experience other realms of reality we move into our seventh sense, our multidimensional awareness. Within that seventh sense there are three basic levels of awareness: *initiation*, in which we become aware of other realities; *communion*, when we begin to intentionally interact with others beyond this reality; and *ascension*, when we can intentionally rejoin our source, the One.

Our energy systems consist of more than just the chakras or energy power points in our bodies. We also have multiple, in fact infinite, layers of energy within and around us. Our fields of energy change as we experience life because they continually communicate with all of creation, which communicates with us at the same time. Our energy fields dictate our emotional, spiritual, mental, physical, and even intuitive experiences. In any given moment we are never quite the same as we were even a moment ago, because our energy fields change in the course of our experiences. Because of this, we are all unique. We are the culmination of our experiences since the beginning. We are everything that we have ever lived.

We are also created of sets of harmonic frequencies. Energetically speaking, we are constructed very much like one gigantic and intricate musical chord, with each plane of reality being a note in that chord. Our harmonic frequencies dictate our presence in third-dimensional reality. They also direct our experiences on Earth, our karmic journeys (which are those lessons we attempt to learn), and the choices we make. Our energy systems continuously evolve in response to our lives, our environments, our world—in fact, to all of creation.

The Indigo Children are so named because of the prevalence of indigo blue color within their energy fields. The little ones in this book, however, have energy fields that have evolved far beyond those of the Indigos and previous generations. The Children of Now exist within living arrays of subtle energy that sweep and swirl, energy that brings to these very special children unlimited awareness, giftedness, and sentience (or "knowing") far beyond what we used to consider "normal." The Children of Now are startling not only in their insights and their giftedness, but also sometimes even in their disabilities. As human beings we have learned by example from our predecessors that "different" is uncomfortable and something to be avoided. We have been taught that we are comfortable when everyone fits into nice, neat boxes and looks and acts like everyone else. Those times are over. The Children of Now are an exciting leap in human evolution.

However, countless Children of Now continue to be overlooked. Although our tendency as a society is to classify and categorize, we do not yet have parameters in which these amazing children fit. That is because these kids resist and shatter restrictive and limiting categories. The Children of Now are not being encouraged or nurtured in ways that their inherent gifts require. Because of this, these children have problems in all aspects of their lives. Many of these special little ones suffer from a different kind of neglect, one that is simply caused by ignorance on the part of parents and caregivers regarding the true nature and source of these children's differences. This is not intentional. Oftentimes, these kids look just like everyone else, but on the inside they are much different than other children. They know things that most people haven't ever thought of (yet may have felt deep within them). As human beings we are often afraid of what we do not understand. For many, religious beliefs, historic records, and social norms and mores suggest that anything or anyone who is different must be ignored, controlled, or hidden. When it comes to the Children of Now, we are doing ourselves and the world a disservice by not acknowledging them!

In earlier generations, as we arrived on the day of our birth, we quickly forgot our origin. We forgot our giftedness, our Source, and our perfection. The Children of Now not only remember much of what we have forgotten, they embody it. It is not my intention to pigeonhole children categorically; rather, it is to explore the phenomenon of the Children of Now and tell their stories. I do so because this phenomenon offers the possibility for positive change in our world. I urge the reader to view the approximate age groups enumerated here loosely, as there are many overlapping situations and transitional energies that create commonalities. No two children are exactly alike, but there are shared traits. The levels of giftedness are individual to each child.

The information contained in this writing may be quite new for many people. A number of these stories will describe facets of reality that may challenge or defy all logic. Some of it may seem quite strange, but it is very real. I have used a variety of examples in each section—some of the examples are extreme, some are not. This is intentional because, as energy and consciousness, we all share identical traits but also carry a myriad of traits that are ours alone.

Some of the stories in this book will definitely challenge your ability to believe, and some will definitely stretch the your perception of reality. In my humble opinion, that is a good thing! My beliefs never included the ideas and events found on these pages until I not only encountered these situations, but lived them. Sometimes the lesson in life is really about letting go of beliefs and looking at the truth for what it is, and not what we want it to be.

Any time our "safe zone" of everyday reality is challenged, we have a tendency to fight back and close our minds, because the unknown can be frightening. I suggest reading this material with an open heart and mind, and with the aim of expanding personal awareness. We cannot grow without challenges that stretch us to greater heights of wisdom and knowledge. Again, it is important to remember that not every child shares the traits discussed herein; just as in biological evolution, there remains a mixed or uneven advancement until new traits spontaneously normalize in the populace.

In my opinion, labels are often inappropriately given to adults and children alike as ways of defining, and hence understanding, different types of behavior. Many of those labels are not only incorrect but ultimately cause damage in the long run. Currently, countless children are being given medical diagnoses such as ADD (attention deficit disorder) and ADHD (attention deficit/hyperactivity disorder). These labels have become catch-all diagnoses for those who do not fit the norm. Worse, with those diagnoses come prescribed medications that dull the children's senses and create a comfortable status quo for everyone else. Or do they?

In some ways, the very different realities that these children bring to our world may feel threatening only because we have no experience on which to base them. I would submit that "normal" is a perception, and that perception is part of our everyday illusion. To move away from illusion our perceptions must change! I do not intend to create more labels; rather, it is my goal to explain a very real phenomenon. Instead of applying labels all around, let us embrace the differences and limitless gifts that the Children of Now bring to our world in the form of knowledge, wisdom, and healing—and even what they remember from far beyond our everyday reality.

This work is a compendium of ongoing research. I am an author and medical intuitive with an international healing practice. I travel widely, lecturing, presenting workshops, and facilitating private healing sessions. Throughout my practice I have encountered child after child who is astonishingly gifted, and yet not only unrecognized, but invalidated—by parents, teachers, and other caregivers who have failed to appreciate the import of their children's differences. Because of this, many of these children have become sick or behaviorally unacceptable. Others are so intellectually, spiritually, and emotionally advanced that they suffer from a great sense of not belonging. They come from a frame of reference that is foreign to most people, and because of this many of these children remain unheard, invalidated, and unacknowledged.

I have encountered and facilitated healing sessions with some of the most astounding children. Each time they have taken me to new and amazing heights of reality. They communicate about subjects that, until recently, seemed to be the stuff born of science fiction. In fact, interactions with the children have taken me far beyond my own scope of imagination. I can guarantee that my imagination is not so great as to have been able to fabricate the stories I am about to tell you! It has been said innumerable times that expectations create reality. We have the tendency to view the Children of Now from old paradigms that no longer apply. It is my intention to counter this tendency by casting light on the Children of Now so that they become not only noticed, but nurtured, enhanced, and honored as well.

My first conscious awareness of a Crystalline Child came with the birth of my granddaughter in 1999. She came into this world with heightened awareness, and immediately after birth quietly observed everything around her. Later, as she lay in my lap, her consciousness attempted to rise up and out of her body as she fought the limitations of her new physical being. I could see her willing herself to get up. The concentration in her little blue eyes was intense, and yet there she was—stuck in her tiny body. I remember laughing and asking her if she was trying to run away. Little did I know then that she was probably used to projecting her consciousness wherever she wanted, and that she was trying to take her new body with her! That was only the beginning. I knew that my granddaughter wasn't alone in her giftedness, and that there were others like her. That realization led me beyond curiosity and into uncharted territories of reality.

Each child, each situation, is different. The information compiled in this book is based upon firsthand experience gleaned from healing sessions, personal interviews, and Websites, as well as input from professionals who also not only recognize these children, but work with them on a daily basis. There are not many books available that discuss the realms that we will encounter in these pages. Where applicable, I have cited those references. There are some great Websites that offer information about the Children of Now, and I have included those at the end of this book to enable you to delve even further into this subject. These lists are not recommendations—they are simply other avenues that appear to offer useful and current information about the children.

It is my passionate intent that this book act as a bringer of awareness and as a support mechanism for parents, teachers, caregivers, educators, and even the medical establishment. Mostly, however, it is for the Children of Now, who are not getting what they need. Many children are suffering unnecessarily just because their needs are not recognized. Some families are simply afraid of the gifts their children display. That fear brings out yet another set of problems as the children grow and mature. When there is such a sense of difference, it is always good to know that we are not alone.

In the interest of not exploiting families and their children, or betraying the implied covenant of confidentiality between counselor and counselee, I have used pseudonyms in place of almost all of the children's names—with the exception of Nicholas, who wrote the beautiful foreword, and Lorrin, John Everett, Peter, and Christina, about whom I will talk a little later. Of course, not all gifted children resemble those described in this book, but you might be surprised at how many do!

It is my desire that everyone who reads this takes away some new piece of information, a glimmer of curiosity, or even a different opinion that will ultimately assist a child who might not have otherwise been recognized.

At the top of each chapter, and in a few other places, I have included direct quotes from some of the children with whom I have come in contact. The simplicity of their messages has moved me beyond words time and again. In many ways, it is as if God, Source, and Spirit are speaking directly through the children. They remember.

When the Children of Now are nurtured and their gifts are encouraged, they continue to remember and share amazing observations and gifts along the way. Sadly, it is my experience that a great number of these kids are denied validation for their stunning disclosures. The children are candid about what they see and experience, but because they are denied support for their gifts, they soon begin to forget what they knew when they came to Earth. Eventually, they stop using their gifts. For instance, one little blond-haired, blue-eyed girl whom I have known since shortly after her birth has delighted and amazed everyone she has met since she could speak (at a very early age). She is about 4 years old at this writing. I will call her "Sky." Since she was tiny, Sky has gathered audiences wherever she goes. With her compelling personality, she is a magnet to humanity. Until recently, as people collected around her, Sky expounded about life, truth, and otherworldly subjects. She is wise beyond her years. She is also gentler and more physically coordinated than most children her age. Sky later became shy with people and generally stopped publicly sharing her profound insights. She was no longer her effervescent self. When she was asked why she decided to be silent, her response was, "When I talk, people laugh at me and it hurts my feelings. I don't like being laughed at, so I quit talking to them." Sky's parents greatly honor her giftedness and even encourage it, but the general public treated her as a spectacle and a novelty, and so she closed her communicative doors. What a loss for us all! Unfortunately, situations such as this are more the norm than not. If they are not nurtured, validated, and encouraged, by age 5 or 6 the children install protective energetic walls around themselves that block the information stream. Soon, most signs of heightened awareness fade, doors to higher consciousness become closed, and all is forgotten. The children are very sensitive about being "different." What a sorrowful statement for us as "enlightened" and "civilized" people! The means to create a more positive world is coming to us in the form of our future generations, and we don't even recognize this. The Children of Now bring us the keys to the secrets of this life and beyond, and we bar the door. *What are we thinking?*

In earlier generations it was taught that children should be seen and not heard. Now more than ever, it is the children to whom we must listen. In the trajectory of our evolution as human beings, the Children of Now are a bridge to higher consciousness and, yes, even the future of this planet. How will we recognize them? Will we listen to what they have to say? Can we take the leap, knowing that these children can take us far beyond our current perceptions of reality and into exciting new realms of awareness and possibilities? It is up to us as their mentors, caregivers, and families to take notice of these children, and to take action on their behalf. We must set aside old paradigms and open our hearts, our minds, and our souls to the possibilities that the Children of Now have to share with us.

We have an opportunity before us like nothing we have ever seen or experienced in the history of humanity. In my opinion, awareness is about 80 percent of the solution to any situation. To find this awareness, we must first accept the possibility that there is more to our reality than we currently know or accept. This phenomenon crosses all boundaries of race and religion, and, in fact, all measurable belief systems and social norms. As Nicholas so eloquently states in the foreword, we must deeply listen to the children. Further, we must be willing to open ourselves to what their messages convey.

When we look around at our current world with honest eyes, we begin to realize that both humanity and the planet on which we live are on a course of destruction. We have forgotten the wonders of existence beyond everyday life. We forget to notice the perfection of each moment in which we exist at any given time. We look outside ourselves for comfort and gain, and often expect that someone else is responsible for giving us what we need. In general, we are people who have a great sense of emptiness, and we strive every day to fill it. What we have forgotten is that we are already full. There is nothing that we need that is not already within us. The children remember this, and they have come to remind us that we are much greater people than what we experience in the everyday illusion called "reality."

The Children of Now bring possibilities of remarkable evolutionary change to our world. They have a mission and an immense purpose, and they need our help. Their giftedness brings enlightenment to us, and their wisdom offers reminders of times and worlds we have forgotten. The Children of Now are not only on a mission to teach us about greater reality from within their innocence and their clarity of truth; they are also the future of our world. In fact, if we pay attention to the Children of Now, the future of humanity can change direction from the destructive path it is currently on to a much enhanced, much more positive reality—one that is more globally oriented and offers the highest benefit for everyone.

The bright stars you will find in these pages are in many ways miraculous. They defy all behavioral and psychological boundaries, crossing societal norms and religious beliefs. They are bridges to all humanity from our Source, and bring important messages to us. The Children of Now are the spirit of perfection—beacons of light filled with passionate truth and the innocence of what humanity once was and can be again. The children are here and they are now—and there are more on the way! Are we ready to pay attention?

CHANGES *in* EVOLUTION

CHAPTER 1

---

*Creating a new reality in this world
is as simple as doing it.*
(A telepathic message from one of the children)

Why are so many children being born right now with special gifts? Why are they "different" from other people? *How* are they different?

Humanity is moving through a circular evolution. As described more fully in my book, *Pyramids of Light: Awakening to Multi-Dimensional Realities,* our electromagnetic energy fields and our genetic structures continually evolve toward our original state, which was light—the same light that is our Source, our God, and our Creator. To some degree, each of us carries that light within us, and that light contains the memories of all time. The memory of that light within our very being drives our evolution back toward our origin.

Before time as we measure it, and during our evolution as human beings, we became denser and denser until we arrived at our present form. During that process, our thinking minds developed because we were faced with the need to survive as biological entities. When we migrated in search of sustenance and because of climate changes, we also had to learn to communicate with others. With that communication developed the art and subtlety of words, and later, our egos. Even now our egos tell us whether we are safe or not based upon our previous experiences. Our egos often lie to us because they don't evaluate our current circumstances in light of the truth of the moment, but only in light of what we have experienced in the past. Because of this, sometimes our logical brains fill in the gaps so that things seem to make sense—and that often gets us into trouble! Like swinging pendulums, we have moved past our most base state of development and are now on the upswing toward our highest existence. As everything within us seeks its Source, changes occur within us.

NEW DNA RELATIONSHIPS

All human beings have a DNA system in which each strand looks like a twisted ladder (see Figure 1). The DNA strand is comprised of segments of proteins that communicate one to each other. The way that these protein filaments have communicated for millennia has been by linear interrelationships among the segments that

Figure 1. A section of a DNA strand.

work much like a chain reaction. One protein segment communicates with another and then another along the chain.

When a change occurs in our body, our RNA carries messages to and from our DNA (see Figure 2). The RNA recognizes events within our bodies that our DNA needs to know about, and carries messages about those events through our body to our DNA, which responds accordingly.

Besides communicating with the protein segments, our DNA has a field of electromagnetic energy between and around the strands that functions like a liquid crystal radio set. This field operates based upon certain sets of frequencies, much like tuning into a radio station. The electromagnetic energy field in and around the DNA transmits and receives data, and tells our bodies and our subtle energy fields which changes are necessary. When we have feelings, physical sensations, emotions—in fact, any experience at all—the entirety of our makeup responds and changes as our electromagnetic system and our RNA tells our DNA about the experience. The messages travel through our subtle energy systems, which communicate infinitely. In other words, *our DNA is talking to all of creation.*

As we communicate to the universe, new realities are created. Our bodies as well as our life experiences change in response to these new realities. If our systems require an adaptation to acclimate to new circumstances, the DNA not only instigates those changes, but monitors them. As it is with our brains (of which we only use about 5 to 7 percent), we use very little of the information that is available within our DNA because we have forgotten how to access it—at least, that is how it used to be. Recently some of us have begun to remember!

In the past few years, our RNA has begun to identify electrical and electromagnetic data that it had previously not been able to recognize, and transmit it within and around the body. In other words, the radio stations have changed frequencies to broader reception bands. This changes the interaction amongst our DNA segments and our body, and hence our relationship to all of creation.

These new patterns that have evolved allow DNA to communicate differently. The Children of Now are living examples of this genetic revolution. Instead of communicating in a linear fashion, the electrical charges that are part of the communication mechanism throughout the DNA ladder have begun to arc from one protein segment to another. As this occurs, the charges often jump from a segment on one DNA strand to one or more segments *on the opposite strand.* This is an amazing new development.

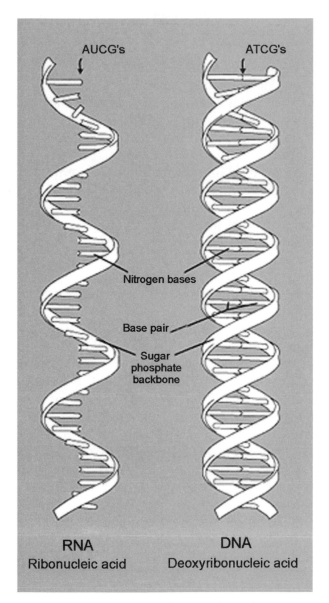

AUCG's

ATCG's

Nitrogen bases

Base pair

Sugar
phosphate
backbone

RNA
Ribonucleic acid

DNA
Deoxyribonucleic acid

Figure 2. RNA and DNA relationships.

As our DNA changes, we evolve. The new patterns of electrical relationships within our DNA create a weaving of energy—a web of electromagnetic energy—*between* the strands that is, for lack of better words, rewiring us. These new genetic relationships create an energetic matrix, a new field of energy between the legs of the ladders of DNA structure. When these fields begin to harmonize and unify, we change, and our children change.

This rewiring is a major leap in our evolution as consciously aware beings. Humanity has begun to awaken to other realities and even to higher states of conscious awareness. We have begun to remember that there is much more to us than what we knew previously. Countless people have spontaneously begun to remember past lives and have become multidimensionally aware. Some find that there are no limits to what can be done with pure consciousness.

As more and more of us "wake up," more and more of us will remember.

As we change, our DNA and RNA continue to adjust in response. As this process occurs, the DNA within more and more people begins to change and evolve even more rapidly. The process is constant. As the DNA transforms within one, then two, then more and more people, there comes a time when there is a consensus of nature. Many people call this critical mass—the moment in time that an evolutionary trend becomes the norm. (By way of illustration, you may recall the "100th monkey theory," which basically states that when more and more people learn to behave differently, there arrives a time when critical mass is reached, and the entire populace spontaneously takes on those behaviors as the norm.)

We have critical mass in consciousness as well. As we evolve physically, the functionality of the consciousness within us grows too. From the standpoint of evolution, this is huge. Not only are our children exhibiting aspects of higher consciousness, but we have begun to see, even in adults, levels of conscious awareness that just a few years ago were unheard of. Because of this, children who are coming into our world as the progeny of our new evolution are arriving with new, more advanced DNA communication patterns.

The new patterns in our DNA system are a lot like the Internet except that they are unlimited in their scope and capabilities. They are infinite, and the scope of our potential is infinite as well. Our consciousness has begun to work more easily and more fully in conjunction with our DNA systems. As fuller universal communication takes place, our consciousness becomes more and more aware.

Our children listen not only with their minds, but with their entire bodies as well. Moreover, their energy fields are attuned to a much broader field of transmission and reception. The Children of Now are communicating within our world with every particle of their being, and the world is talking back. But are we truly hearing our children?

CONSCIOUS AWARENESS, DNA, AND ENERGY

Consciousness is not the mind. The mind is purely a logical construct—a tool we developed that assists in our survival as human beings. As part of our defense system, it rationalizes, quantifies, and informs us of our progress during the course of our experiences. Consciousness is not the ego either; it is the essence of our true selves. It is not stuck within the body and can travel easily to other times, places, and realities in both real time and in dreams. Our consciousness is superluminal (faster than the speed of light), and is able to bring whatever information or experience we want or need from anywhere in creation.

Consciousness is what enters the incipient cells when we are conceived. It carries memories of our previous lifetimes, which is why we have déjà vu. We *have* been there. It is why we know someone even when meeting them for the first time. We *have* known them before. Consciousness is what reaches out beyond the reality of this here and now and brings intuitive information to us about the past, present, and future. It is that part of us that is ever-diligent and aware of everything in all of creation. Our consciousness is capable of moving mountains, changing the form of matter, and traveling in time and space—and even to other realms of reality. It is able to instigate healing on profound levels by reaching into the consciousness of others and feeling and knowing what they experience. It is our greatest power and our deepest sensitivity.

Because we have learned to think and communicate logically, our memory of pure consciousness has become tainted during our evolutionary process. We closed the door to awareness of greater realities as a matter of natural course. Now those doors are reopening as awareness returns to us. The Children of Now arrive in our world with those doors partially or wide open, and their consciousness easily does what we have long since forgotten that ours could do. The children's consciousness remembers who they are and where they have come from, and in turn, that remembering mirrors our true selves.

Because both consciousness and DNA are comprised of electromagnetic energy, they work in tandem. When our consciousness and our DNA work together, we can operate as *intentional conscious observers and participants* within all of creation. Our consciousness experiences every level of reality and then communicates those experiences directly to the DNA electromagnetically. (Remember, our DNA receives data from the RNA, processes it, and then communicates those experiences back through the body again via the RNA.) At the same time, the DNA relays those changes to consciousness and back into all of creation. It is an endless cycle, vital not only to our very existence, but how we experience it as well.

Every thought we have, every word we utter, and every feeling we experience is a form of energy, and thus has a harmonic signature to it. Each signature is a combination of frequencies that, in its completeness, carries specific messages to us and from us. For instance, when we have an experience that is unpleasant, we may have a visceral reaction within our bodies—a leap in our chests or a knot in the pit of our stomachs. Conversely, when we have an experience that is pleasant, our chests "swell up" with the emotions of the moment. Our bodies are reacting to our experiences. As the energy frequencies of each experience are communicated through our bodies, those frequencies don't just affect us physically—they become part of our consciousness. Thus, each experience is recorded or imprinted physically (biologically) and energetically (on our energy fields), and these imprints become part of us and all of creation. Consciousness also communicates directly with DNA, so we are having an etheric and physical existence at once. The result of all of this is that we are no longer as we were the moment before. Our entire makeup has changed, and our energetic, harmonic makeup has adapted to the circumstances. Some of the changes are profound, while others are much more subtle.

The Children of Now have an even more direct, streamlined, and refined universal communication system, one that skips many of the steps that previous generations needed. The children's energy fields are living transmitters and receivers. Because of this, some of the children exhibit what seems to be rare giftedness, such as the psychic children in China who perform amazing feats, or the Indigos who communicate along energetic grid pathways. The new energy systems of the Children of Now are arrays of living energy. This is similar to having a radio on all of the time that is tuned into all of the stations at once. Some of the children can filter out excess unwanted data, some don't need to, and some have learned to process all of the information simultaneously because their brains work differently. To the Children of Now, all channels are accessible at the same time and without adjustment to the instrument. Pan-reception!

Many of the Children of Now exhibit amazing awareness, knowledge, and intuition—in fact, an unlimited array of gifts. They automatically use their consciousness in ways that bring to them and to us answers about life and being beyond time. On the other hand, because of their DNA structure and patterns, the Children of Now are hypersensitive both to their own feelings and to those of the people around them. Their profundity is beyond comprehension, and their compassion informs and energizes their social consciousness. As consciousness embodied— enhanced by the evolution of their DNA—the Children of Now represent a completely new way of being, and they continue to evolve long after they are born. Their energy fields adapt constantly, changing colors and patterns of movement, and becoming lighter and lighter in their overall color spectrums.

Those children who are supported in their giftedness thrive and create fantastic art, music, and science, and provide insight of unlimited depth. They see the truth of our being as humans never have before, and have the ability to express those perceptions with great love and sensitivity. Unfortunately, many of the Children of Now are not being heard. Their profundities are being brushed aside as fantasy or vast imagination. The truth is that their perceptions and experiences are very real!

MEDICAL
MISUNDERSTANDINGS

CHAPTER 2

HARMONICS AND BRAIN FUNCTIONING

When we receive a stimulus of any kind, our brains work by sending electrical impulses that deliver messages along the neural pathways within our brains and throughout our bodies. These messages are also delivered and transmitted to and from our consciousness and all of creation. Our messaging systems work in the form of fields of electromagnetic frequencies, or energy. The energy fields in and around our bodies, and those that exist multidimensionally, are electromagnetic in nature as well. All of our energetic levels of existence communicate constantly with each other. This is a lot like being "online" all of the time, getting whatever information we need in any given moment without effort. Because we use our brains in a logical fashion, we are not generally aware of the more subtle communications that we experience.

Gifted people have brains that function differently. Remember, energy carries information, and the brain uses energy for its operation. People who are intuitive or gifted metaphysically have an innate ability to "tap in" to different levels of subtle energies and therefore other realities, where they experience precognition and, in some cases, free their consciousness enough to explore other times and places, and realities beyond the third dimension. For those who are intuitively or otherwise paranormally gifted, the messages contained within the energy are distributed differently within the brain so that they are understood (at least on some level of awareness) and not lost in linear brain functioning. Not all of this different functioning is visible in medical tests, because the medical community has yet to seriously or fully consider the possibilities or the impact of subtle energies. They do not yet have instruments to measure these finer, more subtle types of energy.

Often, because of certain stimuli or changes within the relationships of energetic functioning, a child of the new evolution may look different or even overtly dysfunctional. In other words, some of the New Children do not appear to function "normally" on a mental, emotional, or physical level. Some of the children experience all manner of apparent disabilities, from minor to substantial. Many of them seem to be profoundly physically disabled while exhibiting a spiritual clarity that demonstrates a mastery and wisdom beyond that of most adults. Those who appear to be profoundly affected often do not or cannot speak, and many communicate telepathically more easily than most of us do with words. Some children also do not behave "normally" as expected in certain situations. Others seem to be "spaced out" or "not with the program." That is because their program is far beyond our simple everyday one.

Some of the children are just "differently able." They are highly intuitive and brilliantly gifted, yet they demonstrate apparent difficulties in linear learning or learning by rote. Because of their high intelligence they often become bored, showing signs of apathy in the form of poor academic performance or disruptive behavioral issues. One reason for this is that, because of the "fast track" nature of evolution at this time, changing or disharmonic energies sometimes become resident within the brain waves and throughout the children's energy fields. The energy relationships within the brain and the overall energy system encounters static, much like when there is interference on a radio station. The energy patterns often begin to function in circular patterns within the brain, and this affects which areas of intelligence can be accessed by the child. Conversely, in some children, the energy fields within the brain unify, creating a field of energy that accesses parts of the brain that most people do not normally use.

Because of these seemingly anomalous energy changes, some of the children display physical dysfunction, general brilliance (or giftedness in a particular subject matter), and even remarkable inherent spiritual insight. The possibilities are limitless, and depend only upon the organization of subtle energy fields within the children's brains.

Although it measures electrical responses in the brain, an electroencephalogram (EEG) will not usually pick up this type of activity. For this reason, many children with these anomalies have normal test results and thus are deemed "medical mysteries." This is because the medical field does not factor in electromagnetic relationships both within and around the bodies, or even the fact that every human being is layer after layer of subtle energy forms and fields. The multidimensional aspects of the children, which are interacting with each other all the time, are also not considered.

New relationships within our energy fields sometimes enable us to access other realities with our consciousness. We have the ability to streamline our universal receptivity, which brings greater awareness to our third-dimensional experience. When brain wave activity responds to electromagnetic changes, sometimes these frequencies unify, creating interesting patterns. Gamma waves, and even some higher frequencies, become more prevalent. Gamma waves are our highest frequency brain waves—they are a far step above theta brain waves, which we access during meditation and our intuitive moments. To date, modern science has not learned enough to explain what happens when gamma waves become more prevalent or dominant within our brains. When our brain waves begin to take on new patterns, consciousness is affected. This doesn't refer to waking or sleeping—but then, in a way it does. We "awaken" to greater realities.

The New Children's consciousness becomes more aware of alternate realities and multidimensional worlds. In fact, eventually their consciousness becomes free of spatial and chronological limitations altogether. These children easily switch from one reality to another, and remain consciously aware of all realities simultaneously. This initial awareness is what I call *initiation*—the state in which our brain wave patterns have unified, and early recognition of otherworldly realities begins. At this stage, there is an awareness that other realities exist, but the experience goes no further. The next step is *communion*, which entails conscious interaction with other realities. The child is not only aware of other realities, but becomes fluently conversant with them. This means seeing and talking to other beings in other planes of reality. (This gives an entirely new meaning to the concept of invisible friends!) Communion also means intentionally experiencing the energies of alter-realities, and even learning from them. The children are able to see and interact with their guides and other etheric beings, and even develop friendships with them. They are able to project their consciousness out into the universal construct to travel in space and time, and become bringers of wisdom to our world from far beyond.

AUTISM

Currently, there are more children being diagnosed with autism than ever before, and the numbers are climbing. Consciousness is an amazing thing that most professionals—in fact, people in general—do not understand. Because of this, medical diagnoses are often made that are, in this writer's opinion, in error.

Sometimes when children are born with such great gifts, and are not recognized or encouraged in their giftedness, they begin to withdraw into their alternate realities. In these cases, the children appear to have gone inward, with partial or complete lack of awareness of their third-dimensional surroundings.

The truth is that it is just easier to relate from a state of pure consciousness than it is to deal with being unheard or unrecognized. It is difficult for these children to put into everyday human language the etheric experiences that their consciousness so easily traverses. Of course, not every diagnosis of autism entails this kind of misapprehension, but is something that occurs more and more often as these exceptional children continue to grace our world.

A standard presentation of differently functioning harmonics is autism. In autism, the pathways of electro-magnetic energy within the brain become caught in a loop. In other words, the energy cycles in a circular or elliptical pattern in a small area of the brain. As some of the energy patterns became circular in functioning, other parts of the energy system, the sensory receptors, get stuck on "go." (Again, it's important to note that not all children who exhibit the traits of autism are of the new evolution. Our discussion here is limited to those children who have the new energy patterns.)

When the electromagnetic communications in the brain begin to loop, the child becomes "stuck" within that narrow margin. The network of neurons within the brain develops a small, restricted format, which in turn limits the ability of the child to interact normally on a third-dimensional level. This is why we see varied levels of autism: minor cases, in which children remain fairly functional but with difficulties; moderately affected children, who are only partially functional but appear to operate in present awareness; and even the savants, who are geniuses in specific areas. Harmonically and energetically, what we think of as autism is often merely a rearrangement of the harmonic relationships within the electromagnetic energy fields within the brain, and perhaps the entire body.

The sensation of touch causes many of these so-called autistic children to feel unsafe. This is because, when touched, they feel everything that other people have ever experienced: their deepest fears and feelings, and the darkness and the light within them. In addition, most autistic children cannot tolerate being restrained in any way, because just being in their bodies is difficult. Some of them can't even stand to wear clothes or shoes. Again, this does not apply to all autistic children, as there are other causes for true autism. However, it is a definite phenomenon within the context of the New Children.

There is one school of thought that contends that the mercury contained in childhood vaccines, in our environment, and even in seafood ingested by expectant mothers has contributed to the rise in autism. Most mercury toxicity in humans does, in fact, come from ingestion of seafood. Another source of mercury toxicity is from the mercury-rich amalgam that dentists use and have used in the making of fillings for our teeth. Over time, the mercury leeches out of the fillings and into our systems.

It is a scientific fact that mercury is highly conductive and can actually be used for creating electrical energy as fuel. When there is electrical conductivity, an electromagnetic field is generated. The electromagnetic field is generally opposite in polarity to the electrical field, with the electrical revolving in one direction and the electromagnetic polarity revolving in the opposite direction. This opposition of polarities creates balance and stability. When both the electrical polarity and the electromagnetic polarity spin in the same direction, however, gateways through time and space are opened, the barriers between our reality and that of other worlds disappear, and gravitational pull no longer exists. This phenomenon is exactly how antigravitational technology works, and how UFOs appear to come and go to and from our world. It is how time travel is achieved and how our consciousness works within this reality and beyond.

Therefore, if there is an excess of mercury present within the physical body, the mercury may be contributive to the malfunction of electromagnetic relationships and patterns within the brain—hence the looping patterns and autism, as well as other anomalous behaviors of the consciousness and cognition. The presence of mercury may actually create a new electromagnetic relationship within the body that causes the order of electrical firing to change and/or communicate differently. When those changes occur, the child manifests a lack of, or a change in, certain behaviors, and is thus considered "abnormal."

In fact, when a child is born with the new energy patterns and more refined electromagnetic systems and then has metal toxicities introduced to his or her system, the toxicity may actually magnify harmonic differences or dysfunction in general, and may contribute greatly to changes in electrical and electromagnetic relationships within their entire physical bodies. New energetic relations are formed, and with that comes a whole new set of issues. Metal toxicity can easily be determined through simple blood tests or from analysis of hair samples, both of which can be ordered through a physician.

ADD AND ADHD

Children who utilize the new brain wave pattern often give an appearance of having attention deficit disorder (ADD), or attention deficit/hyperactivity disorder (ADHD). What that means is that the child appears to have difficulty staying on task, paying attention, or retaining focus. The truth is that the Children of Now do not think in the same fashion as their predecessors. Human beings typically think in a linear fashion, with one thought logically following another in an orderly straight line. Every link in the chain of reason serves a purpose of connecting one piece of information to the next until a story is built that makes logical sense.

The Children of Now have brains that work differently. Instead of using linear logic, they think compartmentally. In order to visualize this, imagine that the brains of these remarkable kids have lots and lots of little drawers in them, and each one of those drawers holds different types of information. The drawers open categorically, often with many opening at once. The result may resemble the symptoms of ADD or ADHD because the child does not seem to stay on any recognizable track, jumping from one thing to another, often at an impressive pace. When they think, the Children of Now are able to leap from one subject to the next, recognizing and storing data for later use or until they have enough information that the totalality of it begins to make sense.

Because of this new pattern of thought and their magnified learning abilities, the Children of Now, particularly the Crystallines and the Star Kids, appear to have ADD or ADHD. The truth is that these children do not need to think about things for long, if at all, because they have already neatly stored the information for future use! Instead of attention deficit/hyperactivity disorder, I chose to see ADHD as the

Ability to go into
Dimensional
Hyper
Drive.

With a consciousness that is freed and unencumbered by belief systems, the Children of Now have the inherent freedom to let their consciousness travel whenever and wherever they wish—while still carrying on in the third dimension!

In addition to being called attention deficit, many of the Children of Now are also given the designation of hyperactive. They are not hyper at all except as a symptom of their experience. When a child is able to gather and store information compartmentally, he or she does so with lightning speed, the process often escaping our notice. Then, while everyone else tries to catch up using their more ponderous linear logic, the gifted child becomes bored and begins to become impatient. The impatience often comes across as misbehavior. The child simply doesn't have enough to keep him or her interested, so he or she bounces around the classroom, the home, or elsewhere. As time goes on, the child becomes generally disruptive.

These kids are not dysfunctional, simply different. Using computers as a metaphor, previous generations are like early computers—still working from DOS programming. Their processors are only able to perform one function in a program at a time in a logical progression until the task is completed. This process is logical and linear, following one line of programming language to another to another. In contrast, the Children of Now operate much like the latest supercomputers, multitasking consciously and intentionally and never losing track of any thread along the way. Their information is processed as pure energy, so there are no delays in the communication process. This process is too fast for words. The children's assimilation technique is superluminal—faster than the speed of light. To them, this fast processing is natural. Many of the children are not consciously aware of their differences; they simply function in the way that they are made.

This seemingly scattered functioning creates a misperception by teachers, parents, and other caregivers that perhaps there is a learning disability or some flaw in the child that he or she cannot follow linear logic. Efforts are made to confine the child to certain societal norms and rules, and those efforts are rewarded with even more disruptive behavior over time. Often these children fall through the cracks of public school systems and are labeled as problem children. Ultimately, the child becomes resentful of a society that cannot or does not understand him or her. The child already feels like a misfit because his or her awareness is far beyond the comprehension of most people. Thus, self-image becomes tainted, behavioral issues appear, depression may set in, and communication dwindles because, after all, no one could hear them anyway. Any number of negative responses may develop—all because a gifted child went unrecognized or discouraged.

Instead of celebrating their differences, we give these children medications to offset the depression and hyperactivity, to elevate their moods or calm them down. With these medications, the children become quieter and more manageable, and they seem to pay more attention, but emotionally, spiritually, and evolutionally they are diminished. It is as if society has determined that these kids are runaway trains, and the only way to control them is to put a brick wall in the tracks in the form of drugs. When the train inevitably hits the wall, is it destroyed— just like the children who are given "meds" so they will behave according to old societal paradigms. When these children are medicated, the doorways to higher consciousness are generally unreachable. The children move from excitement about life to more apathetic perspectives. With medication they require less attention—they are quieter and easier to manage—but what was really resolved?

Someone managed to take the situation "under control." Control—that old paradigm which requires that one or more someones must be in charge at all times. The fact is that control is nothing more than a perception of ego that is not applicable in truth. The idea of control maintains that someone is separate from the whole and has taken it upon him- or herself to impose his or her experiences and perceptions upon another or others. When someone maintains that they are in control, the situation is all about that person and not anyone else. What the controller desires according to his or her frame of reference is not necessarily for the higher good of everyone who is involved. Control is *perceived* power.

One of the greatest truths the Children of Now know without a doubt is that we are all one. We are part of a whole that is greater than any one of us individually. When we begin to set ourselves apart, categorically or otherwise, we have begun to step away from that truth, and the Children of Now know this. When a child knows truth to his or her very core, and adults or even other kids try to make that child live outside of that truth, the child is being asked to betray his or her extraordinary being. He or she is basically being asked to lie and to agree that he or she is separate from the whole. This goes against everything that child knows to be true and, because his or her knowing is so profound, this splintering from the whole is literally painful to the core.

In this writer's opinion, the deficits in these particular children are not in attention, cognitive ability, or social skills; they are societal. Society lacks awareness of this escalating evolution of humanity—it is deficient in attention to these children, it has underprovided educational environments or familial support systems, and it turns a deaf ear to what the children are really saying. Our society, like many others, generally requires a scapegoat to blame for its ineptness, and there are those who are persecuted for doing something out of the ordinary—or conversely, for doing nothing. Our society must change its ways of perceiving the Children of Now, or we will have more and more children fall by the wayside who might otherwise have created a mighty and positive change in our world.

ORBS *are* PEOPLE TOO!

CHAPTER 3

*Sending our consciousness out in the form
of geometric perfection allows us to become
unlimited in space and unhindered by time.
Working like this within the same construct
of which everything is created,
we can't possibly go wrong.*
— The Salamander Orb

WHAT ARE ORBS ANYWAY?

Orbs are spherical-shaped energy fields that often show up in photos or videos. They look very much like a perfectly round bubble that is not hollow inside. Orbs appear to move of their own accord, and are often seen or photographed as multicolored spheres with varying and intricate interior designs. There are conflicting opinions as to their source because orbs are not all from the same place. An orb is, in fact, a method of communication that can cross time, space, dimensions, and even intergalactic boundaries. Some people actually see or feel them.

Skeptics generally say that orbs are nothing more than mere dust particles in the air. However, not all orbs are dust. Over the years I have had many interruptions in my daily tasks by a voice that came seemingly out of nowhere, telling me to "get the camera," "go outside," or "turn around," and *every time* I have followed that guidance, I have obtained photographs of orbs! Many of those photos show actual movement of the orbs by displaying a "tail," or trail of energy, behind them. In a way, they look like little comets crossing the photographic field. Sometimes, the spirit world reveals its presence in orb form or other anomalies in photographs. I have taken orb photos in places that are reputed to be "haunted," and they have been featured in news broadcasts about the locale. Over the years I have met many people who can literally call in the orbs so that they will show up in photos. Control pictures taken prior to the "calling" show nothing, but after they are requested to display themselves, the orbs festively manifest in the next series of photos.

I have always been fascinated by possibilities of what orbs truly mean. After all, when one views this subject from a metaphysical perspective, it takes on an entirely new meaning with unlimited potential. Recently, I discovered that this phenomenon is much more than finding strange and curious anomalies in photographs: orbs embody consciousness! Can this be? Yes, it is true!

Figure 3. Photo of orbs at a Crystalline grid. Courtesy of Mikael Koch.

JOURNEY TO DISCOVERY

The best way to describe this startling discovery is to share how it found me. I am no stranger to odd experiences. In my earlier awakening stages, as I became more aware of my energetic system, my sense of reality changed dramatically. I became greatly aware of a magnitude of different kinds of energy on other planes of reality. Every morning I gave myself time to explore these new and wondrous discoveries. I began to be able see energy, and over time I learned how to manipulate subtle energies through movement and music. As I did this, my ability to perceive greater reality stretched. I found myself having experiences that no one I knew could relate to, and it was frustrating.

Each morning as I worked with the energy I begged aloud for assistance from anyone in the universe who was of the light and who could or would guide me. "Show me," I said. One morning as I performed my daily routine, once again begging for guidance, a brilliant Master materialized before me. He stood in my living room, a living hologram, and his brilliance was stunning! He was very tall with crimson robes and his hair was long and flowing. He radiated light that was at once intense and gentle. That moment was obviously an immediate and irrevocable alteration of this writer's reality! The Master showed me how to use energy in ways that I had not yet considered, and ultimately taught me how to manipulate energy for healing, for manifesting greater reality, and even for learning. Over time there was a succession of different Masters who taught me about such diverse subjects as the universal construct, many of the sciences, healing, and so on. Even now, the Masters guide me in almost every moment. It is similar to always being wireless and online, receiving input in my head about any given subject. Strange, I know, but it is true—and much of what they have told me has been validated scientifically long after I received the information.

It has been an amazing journey in which I learned to trust, be open to the unexpected, and have faith that each moment is perfect no matter what is going on. When I do that, my life takes amazing positive turns, and I am carried by a momentum that is much greater than me. Because of this, my work has taken me from place to place all over the globe to meet and talk with thousands upon thousands of people. Without fail, each encounter teaches me something new. When we decide to let go of perceived control and truly trust the moment, the most astonishing things occur. We begin to experience synchronicity in our lives. Obstacles fall away and cease to exist, and one amazing event leads to another and another. Life begins to look like an infinitely choreographed dance. There are no mere coincidences, only opportunities.

The Masters often give me scientific information that is beyond my comprehension. Generally I have a good idea of what the information is about but it often involves complex data that is outside of my sphere of education. I usually seek to place this kind of information with someone who can take it to its highest use. I have often joked that everyone I need to meet in this regard eventually shows up in my living room. The most amazing people have come at the right time and with the right background or connections for what I had to share in that moment. When I needed information about genetics, for example, a geneticist made an appointment with me; she arrived wondering why she had come. We soon found out! As we talked I began to share with her some of the information I had received about communication changes within human DNA strands. She was quite surprised to hear what the Masters had shown me because scientists had discovered the phenomenon only the week before. I had had the information for two or three years by then. It was great fun to share with her what would be discovered next! Over time we became wonderful friends. Another time, when I was searching for information about certain aspects of nuclear energy, a nuclear engineer showed up for an appointment and I was able to share information with him. (Later on I married him, so it was a two for one!) Rocket scientists have come and gone, biologists, pathologists, naturopaths, homeopaths, acupuncturists, movie producers—you name it, they have come and they will continue to come because *I believe.* I am open to greater realities.

Over the past several years I have received vast information about the Children of Now in various forms. I have worked with countless children and their families and have found that all of this information correlates, and the children themselves have validated the information. The past year in particular has brought so many wondrous new discoveries and experiences that there were things I didn't yet understand, but I do now. James Twyman made a great contribution to our world when he discovered that the Indigo Children communicate psychically along universal grid lines. The Indigos communicate with each other and with other people who are "tuned in" in this fashion, from anywhere and at any time. They are truly amazing. Twyman went on to meet many of the children who had begun to talk with him in this manner, and has done wonders exposing this very real phenomenon to the world. Similarly, some of the Children of Now communicate in a different way that is extraordinary and just as real. A remarkable sequence of events brought me to this breakthrough.

During the summer of 2005, I committed to present at an expo in Spokane, Washington. I have presented there for several consecutive years, and when I do, the audiences generally look forward to my presenting on certain workshop subjects. One particular time, months before the event, the Masters told me that I *had* to talk about the children. I was a bit unsure because, after all, I have never considered myself an authority on kids. I had worked with lots of families but I didn't feel as if I had enough organized, solid, or provable information in order to give a proper public presentation. The Masters were relentless. In my head I heard, "Speak of the children," again and again. They weren't going to let up! (When the Masters want me to do something they do not stop until I agree. Frankly, this can be very annoying at times. I have learned that when they are that persistent I had better pay attention, even if what they say challenges my realm of experience or logic at the time.) Usually, when the Masters push me like that, my life takes a turn to higher ground. I receive more understanding, new ideas, greater connections, and new venues in which to teach—in fact, all kinds of positive outcomes. Resistance is pointless because I ultimately find myself doing exactly what they wanted anyway, and it is always perfect! "Okay," I said finally.

My lecture about the children had been advertised, and it received an overall generous response, both in ticket sales and in those who came to share their stories with me at the expo. I was overrun by people who came to my booth and stopped me in the aisles with stories to tell, questions to ask, and general concerns about specific children. As I became aware of the extent of people's need for information about the Children of Now, I began to get the Masters' point.

The morning before my lecture a woman named Julie stopped by my booth to talk with me. In her hands was a photo album that she couldn't wait to show me. Julie began to tell me her story. She told me that she lived in a small community in Montana and that she was a nurse and medical intuitive. Similar to my experience, Julie was regularly sought out by doctors, lawyers, and other professionals, as well as children and families, regarding her work with certain types of children. Julie shared fantastic stories with me about the children she worked with and how she found them—or rather, how they found her! Julie would "get messages." (I can sure relate to that!) Out of the blue Julie would hear something such as, "Get in the car and drive," and she would do so, having absolutely no idea where she was going. When Julie got to her destination, she would be "told" that she had arrived, so she would walk up to the door and knock. When the door was answered, without hesitation Julie would ask, "Is there a child here?" And there *always* was!

The children were calling to Julie telepathically.

Generally, the children who called to Julie were severely physically disabled. They couldn't speak, and some could not hear or see, so they communicated telepathically. In other words, they reached out with their consciousness in silent communication. At one home she visited, as soon as Julie arrived, one boy gleefully told her (telepathically and with sign language) all about her day right up to the moment she arrived to see him. He knew, in detail, *everything* that she had done, experienced, and felt during the entire day! During these visits, Julie often learned that a child was about to be committed to an institution because he or she was severely disabled, and because of the fact that the high level of care that was needed to support the child's well-being was unavailable at home. Julie generally asked the family or caregivers if they would allow her to work with the child, and generally the answer was yes because the families were desperate for help.

With that much of her story told, Julie opened her photo album and began to show me photos of the children. For the most part the children looked quite normal. It was the anomalies in the photos that got my immediate attention: when photographed, the children displayed energy fields in pictorial form. They exhibited colored orbs that were often filled with sacred geometric patterns, or representations of mathematic formulas such as the Mandelbrot set. When Julie first noticed anomalies in the photographs, she wondered if the orbs were a result of camera problems or something in the air. She felt that there was something much more important going on, so she began to experiment with different types of cameras. She tried digital, 35 mm, and disposable cameras—whatever she had available—and the results were always the same: orbs with geometric patterns and in living color. But these photos were far more complex than the "usual" orb photos. When she asked the children about what she saw in the pictures, they told Julie that they were creating the photo anomalies intentionally! So it turned out that the orbs are intentional projections of consciousness. Upon hearing this, I became very excited. I had suspected as much about the orbs for years, but had not been able to prove my theory— until now.

Each photograph showed distinctive orbs that were unique to the child in the photo, no matter when or where the picture was taken. Each orb in its intricacy was an identifiable energetic representation of that child, and the anomalies were consistent throughout her photo collection. They repeated in photographs in different places while the children and their caregivers participated in different activities. The children were intentionally expressing their energetic signatures. But there was more to come. After the initial pictures were taken, Julie and her friends began to experiment further. One day, they took two of the boys (who were known to communicate with each other telepathically) to different sporting events on opposite sides of town. Photos were then taken of each boy at the same time at their respective locations. *The pictures of both children displayed the exact same orb sets with identical intricately designed interiors.* The boys had blended harmonic frequencies to make a point in pictorial form. This was no accident. I have to admit I was impressed. I asked Julie to present the photos during my lecture, as I thought that they were a valuable addition to the mystery of the New Children. I knew that there was something more to all of this, but I just couldn't grasp it at the time.

The afternoon of my lecture came about. The presentation was to be two hours long. How was I going to fill that time? Did I know enough from my encounters and conversations with the children and their caregivers to make sense in front of an audience? Well, the presentation went beautifully, and I realized that my experiences had brought a wealth of information far beyond what I realized. After lecturing about basic descriptions and traits of the different children, I held an open discussion forum for the audience to contribute their questions, comments, and personal experiences. As we talked, the audience was excited to have the opportunity to share their questions and concerns about children who they knew or had in their families, and I was overwhelmed by their responsiveness. Not only did the allotted two hours disappear quickly, but when our time in the lecture room was up, we continued our discussion out in the hallway for quite a while. Okay, lesson learned. But there was still more to come.

The next morning I awoke feeling a bit strange. When I began to dress for the day I felt literally off-balance and could not help leaning to the right. I closed my eyes and began to assess the origin of my imbalance. I checked my energy fields, and what I found in that moment was a great surprise: I had a brilliant, aqua-colored orb in my field! The orb was embedded in my energy field to the right of my physical body and just below shoulder level. It carried so much energetic intensity that it felt heavy in conjunction with my personal energy field. I had no idea what was going on but I was about to find out.

By the end of the day there were *four* orbs in my field, all on the right and each a different color. One was aqua, one was almost a salmon color, another was golden, and another was pale green. I literally couldn't stand up straight because of the energetic weight of the orbs. Needless to say, this was a bit disconcerting, but, being familiar with unknown phenomena, I just went with it.

I was swamped at the expo that day, but every time I got a chance I "checked in" with myself. The orbs remained throughout the day, and I began to adjust to the intensity of the additional energy within my field. Slowly but surely, I began to straighten up. When I saw Julie briefly that day I told her what was going on and she laughed and said that I had been "initiated." Apparently, after seeing the photos of the children, many people tend to become more aware of the orbs. Beyond that she had no further explanation. Though I had hoped to have more conversations with her, I never saw Julie again. I knew there was a lot more to this than simple awareness. I was fascinated and intrigued, so I watched and I waited.

From Spokane I flew to Sedona, Arizona, to present in a weekend-long conference. I had a couple of days to regenerate before the conference began, and because I had arrived before the other presenters, I had some much-needed alone time. During those two days, more and more orbs came into my awareness and attached to my energy field. I realized that I seemed to be collecting an array of all colors and sizes. As this was a new experience, it was a little while before it occurred to me to be still and open myself to the phenomenon. As I did, I realized that I had picked up hitchhikers.

Each orb carried the consciousness of a different child. And they were talking to me. Oh. My. God.

This was another of those moments in life when I was positive that everything I thought I knew was changing. As when the Masters first appeared, I did a reality check. Was I losing it? No way! This was real. I have to admit that I was blown away by the implications of this experience. As accustomed as I am to strangeness, this was an entirely new occurrence. So I thought, what the heck, and tentatively began to communicate telepathically to the children. I felt a little silly there alone in Arizona talking to the energy in my field, until—they talked back. Wow.

Amazing things began to occur. Not only did the consciousnesses of different children begin to collect within my energy field, but earthly children began to gather around me as well. On every flight the rest of my summer tour (and they were numerous), I was seated next to—in fact, often surrounded by—children of all ages. I was deluged by entire classes, school bands, sports teams, and many other groups, all traveling for different reasons. The same was true in airports and restaurants, and virtually everywhere in public that I went. This was no coincidence. During that time I also found myself having profound conversations with the children regarding a variety of subjects. To me, the escalating experiences felt like pure magic—and I knew there would be more to come!

In early 2006, I conceived of a documentary film about the Children of Now, which was to be based upon this writing. I wanted to share some of the magnificent messages that our very special children bring to this world. Just before I left home for my summer tour, I met Michael Shea, who is producing a movie about what happens between our lives. Because I had full sensory multi-dimensional awareness, Michael had hired me as a personal consultant for the special effects in the film. Michael and I had a long phone conversation while I was in Sedona. We were planning some of the preproduction events that happen in the course of making a film. During our talk, I told Michael about the child orbs, which were by then talking to me, and about my plan for a film about the children. Michael became very excited as I recounted my experiences. He asked, "Why not write your movie into mine?" Was I ever excited! I really wanted to help people see what there is beyond the illusion of everyday life, and I also wanted people to see how these very fragile and extraordinary children do not get everything that they need. And now, here was the opportunity to do it all! "Yes!" I replied unequivocally. Long story short, I became cowriter of the screenplay with Michael. There is even a sequel planned as well.

Not only are the children influencing my life, but they are assisting with the script as well. After I got off the phone with Michael, I began talking telepathically to the orbs, the children who were hovering with me. Of course they had heard what had just happened in my phone exchange with Michael. I asked them if they would help with the screenplay. (It hadn't yet occurred to me that this was precisely one of the reasons they had showed up!) Later, I sat at my computer and told the child orbs that it was a great time to talk because I could now give them my full attention and type their messages so that I would remember them. I wanted to be able to take notes and record their messages. I asked the orbs, the children, what they wanted me to say in the book, and what they wanted to be shown in the film. They began to tell me, sharing their philosophies and observations of our world and beyond. The children also showed me worlds of magical scenes that we later wrote into the script. Along the way I asked them questions about humankind and beyond. Here is just some of what they had to say:

ABOUT LIFE ON EARTH

- ✦ *I remember what it was like before I came here. Everyone told the truth and no one ever got hurt.*

- ✦ *Nothing on Earth is as important as everyone thinks. Those are the little things. Forever is what really matters.*

- ✦ *How come people don't remember when things were perfect? They still are, you know.*

ABOUT RELATIONSHIPS

✦ *I wish people could see what they are doing to each other. Maybe then they would learn to treat each other better.*

✦ *Being love is a lot different than thinking about it.*

✦ *So many people seem unhappy. That is because they don't remember who they really are....*

ABOUT TIME

✦ *Think about this: What if yesterday was now and tomorrow was too? Wouldn't that mean that now is always? It is, you know.*

ABOUT FREEDOM OF SELF

✦ *Last night I thought I dreamed that I could fly and then I realized and I wasn't dreaming at all and I really could fly.*

When one's reality changes in such dramatic ways, it is a good idea to use discernment and give yourself what I call a "reality check." I do this often because, for me, reality has a tendency to change frequently! So I told my little orb friends that their orb forms were fantastic, and that I would also love to meet them in their earthly bodies if they were indeed here. Little did I realize what would happen next!

WILLIAM

Shortly after my request to meet the children connected to the orbs, I had an appointment to share a reading with a new client whom I had never met. People often make their appointments with me via e-mail because of my monthly newsletter, "Online Messages." Usually we have not met in person or talked on the phone prior to our session. At the appointed time the phone rang, and there was a delightful woman on the other end of the line. She began our conversation by apologizing. She said that the session was really not really for her, but for her 11-year-old son who does not speak and has other physical issues as well. The appointment was at his request.

As she began to tell me about William, there was chattering in my field. The orbs became very excited, and, being unable to help it, I laughed out loud. "I wonder," I said to this mom (with no further explanation), "if William is one of the children who is talking to me." And then she started to laugh too. She said *she* wondered if I would say anything because her son had told her that he and I had been talking for a while now. Wow. WOW. Well, I did ask for it, didn't I? That appointment actually began a fascinating and endearing relationship between William, his mom, and me that continues to this day.

After our session I had the presence of mind to access the orbs that were still hanging about in my field and ask, "Which one of you is William?" He identified himself as the light salmon-colored orb that was just above my head. Life had just gotten even stranger, but at the same time it was finally beginning to make sense. Since our fateful meeting, William and I have shared some very special moments, which you will read about in Chapter 9. At first I chose to share the orb phenomenon with a very select few, opening their awareness to the phenomenon, but as I did, they began to experience it too!

DILLON

My friend Pam, a gifted medical intuitive, healer, and shaman was called upon to work with a boy who had become very sick after Hurricane Katrina devastated the Gulf Coast. I will call him "Dillon." Dillon became very sick after returning to his devastated neighborhood after the hurricane. He and several family members went back to the area to help others and to check on the condition of their home, which was completely ruined. During the trek through contaminated floodwaters, the family came upon horror after horror of groups of floating corpses. About a week after the family journey to their neighborhood, Dillon became very sick. He spiked a temperature of over a 106° F and was soon hospitalized. When Dillon continued to decline, and regular medical testing did not reveal the source of his affliction, one of his teachers contacted Pam. Dillon was a very healthy child before the storm, and his illness was a mystery to those who tried to care for him. He soon went into a coma and was unable to communicate in the usual ways.

Pam began to talk with Dillon telepathically, and Dillon began to talk back. (Up to that point I had only told Pam that I had the orbs in my field, but I had not revealed to her who or what they were.) Pam became aware of orbs in her energy field that resided just in front of her forehead. As Dillon began to talk with Pam, intuitively she asked him if he was one of the four orbs that she sensed. Yes, of course he was! When she asked Dillon about how they were communicating, he told Pam that when you communicate from within your heart, you give permission to receive communication as well. Basically, by communicating through love, we open all of the doors that, when closed, create resistance to our intuitive selves. Dillon explained that the only reason that the children are able to travel and communicate in this way is because there is a level of purity within them. They are still innocent and haven't put up defenses like most adults. Dillon explained that moving in sphere form allows their consciousness to travel even the tiniest pathways throughout creation safely and without getting lost.

Dillon said that he was uncomfortable in his body because it didn't expand or contract as it used to do in his natural state as an energy body before he came to Earth. He told Pam that being here on Earth is always a choice, and that we can choose to experience it or not. Dillon said that he had chosen not to continue his earthly experience because he wasn't expanding in his lessons as a soul as quickly as he would like, and because he would rather learn and teach from "out there."

As a healer, becoming too emotionally involved with a client can lead to an undesirable outcome. Heartfelt compassion is one thing, but crossing that emotional line creates great vulnerability in the healer, and can even interrupt the purity of the healing. When working with children, it can be very difficult to maintain that neutrality. Pam had quickly become attached to Dillon, even though as a professional she knew that was not a great idea. Concerned about this, Pam asked Dillon why she was unable to avoid the emotional connection with him. His explanation was a magnificent teaching for Pam: "Until now," Dillon said, "you didn't understand the extent of the work that you do. You have an intellectual attachment that is not truth. You must let go of the need for results. Authentic vibration is from the heart and is a very subtle shift. Now you are learning the difference."

Dillon never regained consciousness, and not too much later, he passed away. Dillon talked with Pam throughout his transition. When Pam asked him about his leaving, Dillon said, "The level of the effect of the current collective consciousness of people on Earth goes against the laws of the universe, of all creation. The collective consciousness has become emotionally based. Emotions have nothing to do with creation or destruction, except when you use passion to fuel your intention to manifest reality. A good example is when you pray. You pray with all of your heart and soul, and your prayers are answered. That isn't really emotion. That is creating from pure love. With emotions you can't hold the energy of higher vibration because you aren't in truth. Everything that is mundane must come to a happy place. Just like when you exercise your body, you must exercise your divinity.

Pam was blown away. She said to Dillon, "You are so big!"

He replied, "There is a level of consciousness within you that is beyond emotions and is based on light frequencies, but you bypass that by what you *learn*. You need to initiate balance. This will help change the resonance outward from within your pineal gland, which is the beginning of the river of life."

Pam asked, "Why me, when there are so many others with whom you could have talked?"

Dillon replied, "Pam, when you sought to understand the things that were happening to you, you shouted your name to the universe. You thought you were calling God, but we are *all* God. Many of you can hear us now. You need to listen because we can help you. Those people in your world who are waking up, beginning to remember who they are, they just need to remember. Stop your self-indulgence and do not mourn for me; celebrate me instead! Work on my parents. They are the ones who need you now. Look directly at the orbs who visit you. Your communication with them begins in your frontal lobe. You have opened to them. This isn't a DNA change. Your harmonic signature at this time is a clarion call throughout all the universes. By leaving in this way, I made a choice to affect an entire community by my illness and passing. Lives are forever changed, and everyone who was involved now has a choice of what to do with the experience. This doesn't just affect my family; it affects friends, neighbors, and the entire community. For example, look how meeting me has affected you."

Slowly, communication with Dillon faded as he moved ever farther outward, back to where he wanted to be—and then he was gone.

As more and more of the children contact me, as well as those who can hear them, all of us find that it is quite easy to get in touch with them. The process is similar to sending out a thought and waiting for an answer, and the answer is almost always immediate. The awareness that these children exhibit is stunning; it is as if they are in tune with everything, everywhere, all of the time.

New orbs come and go, and some of them remain with each of us. They are intent upon giving a voice to what they have to say. Many of these children have expressed that it is their sole life purpose to help us remember about love, about who we are, and about the fact that there is much more to being human than our humanity.

The CRYSTALLINE CHILDREN

CHAPTER 4

*What you learn on the outside of yourself
isn't what is important. It is what you learn
from the inside that tells you the truth.*
—Katie, Crystalline, age 6

WHAT IS A CRYSTALLINE?

Why call some children "Crystalline"? Everyone has an energy field, both within them and around them, and as we experience life, our energy fields expand and contract. The colors in our fields vary depending on our energetic makeup, which in turn is based upon harmonic relationships. Color is frequency, and frequency has sound. Through gravitational relationships and energy patterns, all of that sound comes together and creates a unique set of harmonic relationships for each of us. There are no two exactly alike. These harmonic relationships are what make each of us distinctive in all of creation. However, within any given harmonic set, in any person, there are infinite combinations of frequencies.

The harmonic relationships within the Crystalline Children are very different. They carry full-spectrum colors. If you could see their energy fields (which I can!), you would behold arrays of energy, mostly in jewel tones, like magnificent, brilliantly colored rainbows of light. Instead of expanding and contracting their energy fields like their predecessors, the Crystalline Children's energy fields move in a sweeping fashion, much like the searchlights we see spanning the night skies. Imagine having the ability to scan into the ethers with a full set of frequencies!

In my book *Pyramids of Light: Awakening to Multi-Dimensional Realities* (Spirit Light Resources, 2004), I remarked that energy is light and light has memory. We are made of energy and therefore we are light. Light is disseminated in the form of energy. For most of us, our energy, our light, moves through an orderly progression—from the frequency level at which the energy is initially emitted, to the light spectrum in spiral motion—until the energy ultimately becomes white, or perfect, energy. White light contains a full spectrum, and is the same as the energy of the Source—the God energy—or that which is perfection.

The color spectrum is pyramidal in structure, and contains energy that moves in the form of a spiral. The base frequency of the pyramid—and the widest part of the spiral—is red. This would sound as a very low tone, because of the long, slow revolutions of the frequency. If we expend energy starting at the base frequency, that energy will move all the way up the spiral through the entire color spectrum, and will ultimately become each frequency along the way. The energy moves through red,

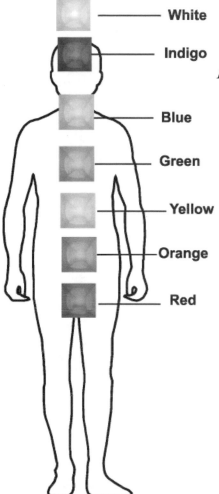

White

Indigo

Blue

Green

Yellow

Orange

Red

Figure 4. The placement and color frequency of the normal chakra system is identical in organization to the spectrum of color found within a spiral.

orange, yellow, green, blue, purple, violet, white, and everything in between. It is no mistake that the colors of our chakra systems correspond exactly to the path of energy frequencies!

The energy fields of the Crystalline Children contain the entire color spectrum. There is a permutation of this pattern, and the children who demonstrate it are often referred to as Children of the Rainbow, or Rainbow Children. There are some subtle differences between the energy fields of the Crystallines and the Rainbows, but in essence they are one and the same. The differences are that the Crystalline energies are extremely vivid in color and movement, while the Rainbow energies are somewhat lighter in intensity, more pastel in color, and more subtle in their movements. Rainbow children are slightly more evolved, with higher, more refined frequency patterns. However, they are so closely related that I consider them part of the same evolutionary trend. For ease of reading, we shall use the designation "Crystalline" for all children in this category.

WHAT MAKES CRYSTALLINES SO SPECIAL?

I remember when there was no time.
I liked that because there was never a bedtime!
—Alec, age 6

The Crystalline Children are fairly new on Earth. They began arriving in 1997 or 1998. That makes them about 8 years old or less at this writing. The Crystalline kids often come to their parents telepathically in dreams, or as a simple "knowing" before they are born. This awareness usually comes to the intended mother of the imminent child. The impending children often name themselves to one or both parents before they are conceived. They often bring other specific messages to their expectant parents as well.

The Crystalline Children create an energy shift as they are born. I know one midwife who has actually seen light appear in the room as these babies are born. Some times this shift is powerful enough to create a temporary sense of imbalance for those who are present at the moment the child is born. Immediately following their delivery, Crystalline babies are generally very calm and alert. They look around the room slowly and deliberately. Their eyes seem to carry the wisdom of the ages. These babies feel at once powerful and peaceful to the observer. They are extremely "present," and often leave onlookers with a distinct impression that they have brought something very special into this world. They have!

Crystalline Children generally (but not always) have very, very blue eyes. Many of them are what I call ice blue. These are the children who look at us when we are in the grocery line or the aisles in Wal-Mart with a look of pure recognition. They are the ones who light up when they spot us and lock us in with a gaze that resonates to our core like a remembrance. When we are captivated by the gaze of Crystalline Children, their eyes convey an essential knowing beyond time and place, and it is usually hard to look away. Some of the Crystalline Children are born nearly fully realized. In other words, they are completely in touch with the etheric worlds beyond this dimension, and have an amazing command of their intuitive, sixth, and even seventh senses. They quickly learn that few others can understand them.

As babies, the Crystallines (like most children) are most often communicated with by their families and caregivers in baby talk and with silly toys. These fragile beings quickly withdraw into their inner world, where they maintain communication and interaction beyond the third dimension.

SWEET ENCOUNTERS, SILENT COMMUNICATIONS

Crystalline babies often reach out to us as if they know us. One day I was in a Wal-Mart in Sedona, Arizona, and there was a little girl sitting in a shopping cart in the same aisle where I was. She was a gorgeous little one with very light, wispy blond hair, and the bluest of eyes. She was maybe about 10 or 11 months old. Her mom was busy looking at shoes and was preoccupied.

When the little girl spotted me, I heard telepathically, "Hi!" I smiled and answered her. We began having a telepathic conversation, and, as we did, she reached out her little hand and grabbed mine—and wouldn't let go. So I just stood there with her. Telepathically I told her that I remembered her too. She smiled hugely and then told me that she was really bored and that her body didn't fit her very well. She said that she felt really stuck because where she came from was a lot "looser." Imagine—she was describing where she was before she came to Earth! We continued our wordless conversation until her mom finally found the items she wanted. As mom prepared to move to another part of the store, she didn't seem to mind the seemingly silent interaction her little girl and I were having, because it appeared that we were just looking at each other and smiling a lot. The baby still wouldn't let go of my hand. After a bit of coaxing, I pried myself loose from her tiny fingers. As we parted, she watched me as she rode down the aisle. As my little friend and her mom rounded the corner, the baby leaned way over and looked around the corner at me, grinning. Her message to me was, "I'll see you later!" This type of interaction is quite common with the Crystallines. They are telepathically gifted and communicate very well if we listen to them.

I was recently at a party at the home of a friend. I had arrived late and everyone was already sitting down to eat in various rooms of the house. As I looked around for a seat, I noticed one in the sunroom and made a beeline for it. As I sat down I noticed that I had landed next to a little girl who sat on her doting grandmother's lap. At first she had her back to me as she played with her grandfather who sat in the next seat. The little one was petite and perfectly shaped, with wispy dark brown hair. She had the mischievous energy of a little elf. Her features didn't have the usual baby fat look to them, so she looked like a tiny adult. As I watched, I could feel the energy field of that darling child. Her force was huge, and came far into my personal space. I quietly tuned into the baby and all of a sudden, as if she had been tapped on the shoulder, she turned around and looked directly at me with her very blue eyes and said telepathically, "Hi!"

"Hi yourself," I replied.

Our interaction went on for about 10 minutes. We had a wonderful conversation about remembering each other and how she was really enjoying all of the attention everyone was giving her. But she wished that people would talk with her about more important things and stop the baby talk. We both laughed aloud, and to many in the room it appeared as if we were having a staring contest. In fact, our interaction made the baby's very conservative grandmother very uncomfortable. At one point she said that her granddaughter was only six months old and didn't know it was impolite to stare. Jolted out of my reverie with my new friend, I was a bit flabbergasted. A baby, rude? Can you imagine? If she had only known! I quietly laughed to myself as I realized that grandma was going to learn a lot from this little girl. No wonder this gifted one had picked this family!

When my granddaughter was about a year and a half old, she spent some time with me at my home. Of course, I was in my glory having such quality one-on-one time with her. One day, we sat on the floor playing with some rather large Lego building blocks. We sat in silence and communicated only telepathically. As my granddaughter looked at me, I would hear, "I want that blue one over there" (or whatever color she wanted), and I would hand that particular one to her. Then it was my turn, and I told her with my mind that I wanted that particular colored one over there. She handed the correct one to me in silence. I was so excited I could hardly contain myself. This went on for about half an hour. I got more and more excited as the time passed while we maintained our silent but perfect communication, and I began to think of all of the possibilities that my granddaughter carried within her. In doing so, I lost my focus. I reached over and randomly picked up a block and handed it to her. For the first time since we sat down, she said, "Memaw, *that isn't the one I told you I wanted!*" The sound of her voice jarred me after such a long silence—she really put me in my place! I had to laugh and hand her the correct block.

GIFTS AND SORROWS

The Crystalline Children are extremely intuitive and cognizant of their feelings. They are exceptionally energetically sensitive. They feel everything that everyone around them experiences—the energy of emotions, people's intentions, motivations, everything. Most of the time they know how we feel before we do! They also have an inclination to be empathic, which means that they literally feel the pain of other people, either emotionally or physically. Because of this, they are the peacemakers. When others hurt, they hurt, so they do their best to maintain balance in their relationships and surroundings. Conflict is extremely destructive to these children, and they will do everything possible to avoid circumstances of conflict.

Because of their sensitivity, the Crystallines have a tendency to become suddenly ill, often with high fevers or odd maladies that don't seem to make medical sense. That is because they aren't just aware; in fact, they experience everything to their cores. Almost every feeling they have is profound. Because a lot of the children are not recognized for who they are, they are either ignored or patronized, and they end up tucking their feelings away deep inside. Their pain then manifests in physical ways, such as unexplained illness, because they have held in more than they can handle.

On a more positive note, I have seen many of these children with a command of healing that is instantaneous and subtle, and yet with an innate power that is impressive. And they do this naturally—without a word, with a tender touch, or sometimes even with just a look. Some of them can instigate spontaneous and immediate healing with a glance. A great example of this can be found in an excerpt from an e-mail I received from the grandmother of a Crystalline boy:

> I did observe Michael again at 18 months of age conduct a healing. My daughter-in-law has a very large family…. A great Aunt was visiting from California. Auntie had been in an accident that resulted in a shoulder injury which required surgery. Her sister (Michael's other "Nanna") was massaging the aunt's shoulder as Michael and I engaged in play on the other side of the living room. There was no indication that this wee one was paying any attention to that which was transpiring on the other side of the room. When the massage was complete, Michael, very deliberately walked over to his aunt and, with great purpose, gently stroked the scarred area with his little hand. He returned two more times to tenderly complete his healing. The other nanna and auntie sat in amazement. I smiled, knowing that I had observed this little Golden (he has blonde curly hair) doing exactly that which comes naturally.

MEMORIES OF GIFTS AND OTHER LIVES

Other children have demonstrated an amazing understanding of energy manipulation. My granddaughter showed this remembering in a remarkable way. On one occasion, when music began to play, it was as if someone had flipped a switch. Automatically she closed her eyes and her hands moved together slowly, fluidly, and intentionally, as if she was about to offer a prayer. As her hands came together, her body began to move with the music. She danced so intentionally, so gracefully, that it almost appeared to be otherworldly. Her coordination was far beyond what we would consider "normal development" for a small child. It was magic to behold. As she did this, she began to shift and flow with the energy in her body and surroundings, her little body moving fluidly as if it were a part of the wind and the currents of creation. It was the most beautiful thing I had ever seen! She seemed to have an innate mastery of something that looked a lot like t'ai chi. As she moved, it was like watching living grace. Everyone in the area became mesmerized. Strangers and friends alike ceased what they were doing to watch her, and conversations stopped. The little Master appeared to *become* the energy, as her hands and body moved elegantly, deliberately, and with an exhibition of oneness that is rarely seen on Earth. It was natural, unencumbered truth in movement. As she gathered energy with her hands and body, she commanded it gently to move and change, and everyone around her could feel the changes.

On another occasion there was a holiday gathering outside. There was a band playing and hundreds of people milling about in the park. It began to rain very hard, and everyone scrambled to take cover. All except the little Master, who once again brought her hands together, closed her eyes and from my vantage point, became an intentional part of the music, the rain, the Earth, and the sky. She danced there on the hill, drenched in the pouring rain, oblivious to everyone and everything else! Watching her, it was as if she had transformed to another place and time. It was such a beautiful moment that I stood there and cried. And where was my camera when I needed it?

Crystalline Children are of the heart. They are greatly compassionate and have an ingrained sense of fairness. They always seem to have the common good of everyone in their motives. On the other side of the coin, when they are dishonored, their sense of betrayal is huge. They cannot comprehend why anyone would treat them with anything other than perfect respect and understanding, and they take any perceived affront very personally. The Crystallines seem to feel personally responsible for the feelings of others, and they harbor those feelings very deeply. They are also quite socially conscious and compassionate beyond their years.

I spoke to one mom recently who wanted to share stories about her wonderful children with me. Margi recognized her children's giftedness early on and has kept an ongoing journal. She asked me what I wanted for my research, and I told her that what I wanted most were descriptions of the children's extraordinary gifts, stories about how they see the world, and descriptions of the profound things that they have said and done that were beyond what one usually experiences with children. Margi began to tell me a wonderful story about her son Peter. One day his school called her at home and said that they were having a food drive. She said something like, "Sure, that will be fine. I will pitch in." But the principal said, "Wait a minute, you don't understand what I am saying: it was Peter who began this project!" Margi was flabbergasted. Peter was about 11 years old at the time. When Margi commended Peter for what he had done, he explained his philosophy that, while most of his family and schoolmates had everything that they needed, others did not, and if everyone would share what they had then all would benefit!

My 6-year-old granddaughter called me at home one afternoon to tell me that she had written a note to her teacher. I said that was nice, thinking that she was being her usual thoughtful self. She went on to say that the reason that she wrote the note to her teacher was because she noticed that the teacher was stressed because it had been a hard day in the classroom. Apparently a group of the children in the class misbehaved, not paying attention to the teacher and it was very disruptive. The teacher had obviously become short tempered. My granddaughter said that she laughed when she gave the note to her teacher, and then the teacher laughed too and wasn't stressed anymore. The note had served great purpose: it brought levity and humor to the situation, and changed the energy of it from tension to lightness. This type of behavior is typical of Crystalline Children.

The Crystalline Children are socially conscious and aware. They are unequivocally the peacemakers. They have a great sense of fairness that generally comes with the wisdom of experience and maturity, and they often put this into action without the guidance or encouragement of others, and to the amazement of many!

While not as common, psychokinesis (moving things with the mind) and teleportation (disappearing from one location and reappearing in another) are other gifts that the Crystalline Children occasionally exhibit. I received an e-mail from one grandmother whose daughter, a young mom, had a new baby at home. What she told me was beyond amazing. The new mom and dad put the baby in her crib for the night and they went to bed. Sometime during the night they awoke to find the little one snuggled between them! Neither of the parents had gotten out of bed during the night! The baby had teleported into mom and dad's bed on her own!

How many of us had invisible friends when we were small? Or have watched our children interact with theirs? Are they really just imagination, or is there something else going on? Most of the children who we will explore in this writing are capable of seeing "through the veils." This means that their awareness is not restricted to this dimension or local reality (by "local" I mean here and now in the third dimension). Time and again I meet children and hear stories from caregivers, parents, teachers, and others about the marvelous interactions the Crystalline Children have with their "invisible friends." The truth is that these friends are only invisible because the average mind has not opened enough to see the way that the children can see.

One little girl I know began talking to the angels when she was a little over a year old. On many occasions she would point around the room (usually at the ceiling) and say, "There is an angel right there and it is a girl one. There is another one over there and it is a boy. They are here watching us." Generally there were several angels present at any given time. This went on for a while until her mother, frightened of the child's abilities, discouraged her by telling her that the angels weren't real. The little one's response was, "Oh yes they are! I really did see those angels. They saw me too!"

Other children can be seen or heard conversing with various otherworldly beings. Some of the kids speak languages that are not of this Earth. In fact, on several occasions I have witnessed two or more of these gifted little beings speaking in otherworldly languages to each other! It is as if they have recognized each other from another time and place and revert to their ancient language. One mom sent this wonderful story in an e-mail to me:

> I sent you pix and info on my granddaughter,
> Malia, who will be 4 on 9/25. I try to talk to
> her about her imaginary friends (and boy does
> she have them). I ask where they came from
> and she'll say they died and came from heaven.
> She has two that she talks about the most—
> Donna and Hebee. She has stories about them
> all, their parents and families.... They are
> frequently there with us at her house or at my
> house when she's over. I act like I know they are
> there and see them and will talk to them too.

The Crystalline Children usually hear and see their etheric guides as if these guides are present in the third dimension. Along with the children's interaction with other worlds comes great and deep knowing of life and existence. They are wise beyond imagination. These children have no concept of being different from the Masters and guides who come to them. And to them this is no big deal because it is normal for them. One of my favorite stories in this vein involves the little boy who ran to his mom and dad's bedroom late at night, and very excitedly proclaimed that Jesus had just appeared to him and explained in detail how the universe works. Excitedly, the boy's mom asked him what Jesus had said, and when she got no reply, she looked toward him and realized that the boy had instantly gone back to sleep! No, it wasn't a dream—and the entire experience was no big deal to the boy because he experiences those types of events all of the time. Mom was a bit beside herself!

Here is another great story from a mom in New Zealand. (I had the pleasure of staying in her home when I did a teaching tour in New Zealand, and I loved getting to know her child.)

One day I was walking with her and we saw a beautiful rainbow. She leapt up from the push chair [stroller] and said with joy, "Look Mom! It's God's promise!" Another day we were playing at home with clay when she looked up at me and said, "You know Mom, God is not a man or a woman. God is a great big ball of light and when you are born, he takes a little piece of that light and gives it to you." This is my favorite story. I was learning a new form of energy pattern massage through a series of weekend workshops. One of our activities was to connect with our animal totems and move with that energy. I found myself linking into the eagle. But something was wrong. I could not lift my wings. I could not fly. This disturbed me and I began to wonder what could be holding me back. It was as if something had tied my arms down. I consulted my teacher and we decided to do a personal healing session to see what we could do about it. During the session, I truly did have a negative energy holding me down. It took some powerful work and I had to literally eat Udi (sacred ash) to remove this force. Both myself and my teacher felt it go. We were both happy about the session and agreed that I should take a music tape with an ancient chant on it to help cleanse my house too. I believe the chant was Sanskrit. I did not know the words. That night as I was tucking my little crystal girl in I played the tape for her. When I tuck her in at night she is normally alert for a long time and doesn't sleep easily. I was amazed when in the midst of fiddling with her teddy she suddenly stopped and began to sing the chant. She knew the words perfectly! She sang with her eyes in a glassy but peaceful stare. I sat there with my chin dropping in awe when she suddenly

> stopped and looked me straight in the eye and
> said, "Mommy you've got your wings now. You
> can fly." Her eyes twinkled and she leaned
> forward with a smile and whispered, "So can I."
> She then settled off to a deep and peaceful sleep
> while I tried to pick my chin off the floor.

The unveiled sight is not limited to angels and etheric guides. Because they are multidimensionally aware, some of the children are able to consciously tap into just about any plane of existence. Remember when we were children and we thought there were monsters in our room? When mom and dad had to come in and close the closet, tuck the curtains snugly around the windows, or look under the bed and assure us that there was nothing else in our rooms with us? Recently I have heard of numerous children who have seemingly irrational fears at night about their bedrooms or other rooms in the house. The number of little ones who experience this is on the rise, because more and more kids have this higher consciousness. They are aware not only of this reality, but others as well; they see and feel other worlds, otherworldly beings, and altered realities, and they know things that they could not possibly have overheard or been taught. We had better pay attention to them! They really do know what they are talking about. Just because most adult people don't experience those things doesn't make them less real.

Because of their giftedness, the Crystalline Children also do not think the same way as other humans do. Instead, they think in the same way their energy moves— holographically and compartmentally, interacting with others and their environments like living sponges. Information goes in and is applied to the compartment in the mind that is most relevant to the input. When fragments of information that do not seem to make sense come into their awareness, these kids automatically store those fragments for future reference. When they find another piece of the puzzle, they store that as well, doing so until a full picture emerges.

Because of their different way of processing data, huge numbers of children are completely misunderstood. Many of these children are put on drugs such as Ritalin to calm them down and focus their attention. Drugs are not the answer. The fact is that we are not raising these children in a way that takes into account the levels of awareness they have. Instead, we have been trying to put them into little boxes of social expectations based upon norms that cannot and do not apply to them. It is time for a change. We must apply new and different paradigms in order to nurture the giftedness of these kids.

I am often asked by parents or caregivers to facilitate healing with children who do not easily fit into their environments. Generally I find that the children have damaged or entirely unique energy fields because of their high sensitivities, and generally it is the people around them who are causing the problems—from nothing more than a simple lack of awareness. Once I work with the families, creating awareness and teaching them how to support their gifted children, most parents stop pressuring the children to fit into those neat little boxes, and everyone feels more at ease. Usually this is because the parents finally realize that there is nothing wrong with their child, but that he or she is instead a gifted being with much to offer the world! With the pressure off, the children become free to be who they truly are, and begin to display even further giftedness.

The children described in this book are not prepared to fit into socially predetermined boxes—indeed, they cannot. Drugs do not change who the children are; they just numb them to their differences. Over time, as the children become discouraged and do not use their gifts, many begin to forget them as they are forced to comply with what is "normal." Soon, they close the doors to other realities and become much like other children. In the worst-case scenarios, this type of oppression can cause problems later as the children grow older. They may develop self-worth issues, depression, feelings of insignificance, or an inward conviction that all is not right in our world. We must remember that, in our new evolutionary processes, there is nothing "normal." The very idea of reality is inextricably linked to the perspective of the person experiencing it. When parents, teachers, caregivers, and so on have an unbending perception of what normal is, these kids don't stand a chance!

The Crystalline Children think so fast that they often seem to skip from one subject to the next, which makes it difficult for everyone else to keep up. They are hyperaware—deeply feeling and lightning fast in their reactivity. They can't be fooled. One afternoon, when my granddaughter was 5 years old, we were having a serious conversation. During the course of our talk I became preoccupied for a moment. Something outside of the window had gotten my attention. My sweet girl was in the process of asking me about something that she felt was very important. When I was jolted out of my reverie, she was looking at me with that "there-is-nothing-you-can-hide-from-me" look in her crystal blue eyes. Preoccupied, I answered her question from a reflexive "adult" perspective, rather than from what was in my heart, had I taken the time to look. Sometimes to an adult, a simple answer is much easier than a long discussion. My granddaughter said, "You didn't tell me the truth. I saw it go through your head and right through your eyes!" I was caught, and frankly a bit embarrassed. She was absolutely right. I apologized and told her what I had really felt. I won't do that again!

Crystallines are generally well balanced in the left and right areas of their brains. They are generally highly intelligent, yet approach matters from a genuine sense of fairness and completely from the heart. They do not have much patience for linear reasoning because they comprehend the entire picture instantly, in spite of all of the details. They are also very likely to come up with profound observations out of the blue. Here are a few examples from children I have known:

+ *Life is not about things and stuff. It is about loving ourselves and each other as much as we can.*

+ *I wish people could understand that when they get mad or happy or sad that they really share those feelings with everyone around them. Feelings are energy and energy moves.*

+ *If God is in me, then I must be God too. That means that I really am the master of all my creation!*

Normal classroom circumstances are quite difficult for the Crystallines, firstly because they are expected to sit still and learn by rote. Because this is impossible for them, this leads to social issues when the children act out in frustration. They are conceptual thinkers and have the ability to grasp information entirely without the need for word-for-word instructions. Remember, they are aware of everyone and everything. They already have vast amounts of input that most of us don't have. Secondly, most school environments still feel very institutional, no matter what kinds of decorations go on the walls. To these children, institutional environments feel hard and unwelcoming. Finally, because of their ability to multitask, the Crystalline Children can appear to be scattered. They flit from one activity to another and don't always finish one thing before going on to the next. They tend to leave a trail of their toys and other items wherever something else got their attention. It can be maddening for teachers and parents to keep up!

Diet is another issue. The Crystallines tend to eat more like birds than people. They like to "graze"—eating little bits more often, and really have no use for sitting down and sharing a full meal. A three-course dinner is often too much for them and makes them feel ill. Many of these kids are very picky about certain foods. They seem to know what they need. We will discuss this more later.

Memories of past lives and "home" are prevalent among the Crystalline Children. At one time or another, almost all of the Crystallines have expressed the desire to "go home." Their parents tell them, "But honey, you *are* home," and the kids will assure their parents that, in fact, they are *not*. One mom asked her son what he remembered about "home," after he had asked yet again when he could return. He said, "What I remember the most was that I was so free!" Another told her earthly dad, "I remember my real father—he never dies."

When we study metaphysics, we are often told that we choose our lives and pick our parents. One often wonders if that information is truth or someone's version of imagined reality. After spending time with these kids, however, there can be no doubt whatsoever that there is something fantastic going on. One of my favorite Crystalline quotes is from a gentle and very gifted girl, Christina, who said this when she was very young: "When I was choosing my new family from 'up there' I looked at lots of people, but I knew you were really nice people so I picked you."

I know her mom. She was right!

NICHOLAS

(Nicholas Tschense wrote the foreword for this book. His insight and beauty radiate from his heart outward to humanity, and I am honored beyond words to have his words grace these pages. All of his writings have been included with permission of Nicholas and his family, who retain and reserve all rights copyright and otherwise to Nicholas's work.)

Figure 5. Nicholas.

Nicholas entered my life about the same time as the orbs began to come to my attention. As I researched online, a synchronistic series of links on the Web led me to Nicholas's Website. The reference to that Website was not in a place I would have expected, and it stood out as a familiar beacon that immediately summoned my attention.

When I clicked on his link, the first thing I saw was Nicholas's photograph. What I saw, what I felt, was a child who is full of love and filled with grace. My heart was instantly and irrevocably stolen! It was as if Nicholas and I had known each other for all time. Via e-mail and through his mom, Susan, we bonded immediately.

My friend Nicholas is an extremely special being. A true Crystalline Child, his purpose in life is to teach people about love. Because he does not speak in words, Nicholas communicates eloquently through his writings. He writes words of wonder and beauty, and has done so since he was a toddler. Nicholas carries wisdom from unfathomable depths of his deepest heart and greatest love outward to the world. His messages remind us that we are much more than isolated fragments of individualized humanity. His words remind us of our oneness, and the importance of being in touch with this oneness. They portray the greatest truths and his expression of them is gently spoken. Nicholas has touched many people to their core. When he writes, Nicholas plucks words from the light of heaven and brings them forth as human language. His is the truth of the One.

When he was 4, Nicholas wrote the following poem (with a little spelling help from a friend):

Love Moves Me
Love is beautiful,
Love is calming,
Love is touching
As it travels me!
On the inside of my body
it moves me
and I am alive,
My being is one.

(By Nicholas M. Tschense. Facilitated by his friend Laura Batson. All rights reserved by Nicholas and his family.)

Nicholas *is* love. He is a bridge between humanity and the heavens, and he does this shamelessly and with great sincerity. He us unafraid to tell the world about what he knows and his gifts are priceless. At age 6, Nicholas presented the following speech to an audience of more than 200 people at the 5th World Congress on Qigong, and received a standing ovation. Moments before presenting this speech, Nicholas received an award for his contribution to the Child and Youth Project for Healing and Peace.

WHY DO HUMANS REQUIRE NATURE AS HEALER?

Nature is the best way to achieve harmony. Nature represents God's love and perfect order. When one communes with nature it may take some time to feel its full presence, but believe me it is all there. Nature has its wondrous beauty. It has the fully ordered divine presence of God. It is so remarkable how God has given us this gift. It is there for healing and admiration. We must approach it with the greatest of love and benediction. Then once nature feels the love, it will continue to offer us its great reward of sustainable life. Healing comes from within; therefore our reference point must be the power coming from divine nature and God, which for me is almost the same. Healing comes from nature and meditation. Meditation is the answer. It brings about the greatest of knowledge. It brings about the universal intelligence where we can all borrow from this lending library. Intelligence offers everything we are seeking. It can be found here. So next time you turn on the television to tune out, instead meditate to tune in to your infinite power and healing potential. Thank you all for being my guests!

Love,
Nicholas

Nine years of age at this writing, Nicholas is off to a great start toward bringing change to this world. He is one of our New Children who have infinite love and unbounded wisdom to offer us. He asks only that we listen and learn that love is truly the answer to our questions. We are listening, Nicholas. Deeply.

PETE

Story after story about the Crystallines remembering their past lives and their time in "heaven" abound. One of these involves a little boy I will call Pete. Pete is about 6 years old at this writing. Pete is genuinely multi-dimensionally aware, as are many of the Crystalline Children.

Recently, as his dad was tucking him in for the night, Pete said, "Look Dad! Do you see the men coming through the ceiling?"

Dad said, "Well, I don't see them, but I believe you."

Pete replied, "Well Dad, they're from the close dimension—not the really far one, but the close one."

One day a couple of years ago, Pete approached his dad and told him that he needed to take a class to learn to speak Chinese. He said that he already knew how, but he just needed help remembering. He went on to tell his current parents that he had been a child emperor in China, and from the details he gave his parents they were able to verify his story from historic records. Pete did get his Chinese lessons and was almost immediately fluent in the language! Way to go mom and dad!

Alec, another gifted child and a friend of Pete's, was visiting Pete and his parents one day. He told them a dramatic story about how he and Pete had lived in Peru together. Alec shared what their names were at that time and how they had hidden in a hotel room. As they secreted away, a gang of men with guns went charging in and shot Pete and Alec to death. Alec's story was full of enough details that his mom was later able to research the details and verify the story. Apparently there was a political uprising in Peru at the time that Alec had described. It may be difficult for a parent to imagine that his or her child has lived other exciting lifetimes before coming back to Earth as his or her child.

The Crystalline Children have great purpose and are willing to clearly tell anyone who listens what that purpose is: to bring unconditional love back to humanity and help instill world peace by bringing the awareness of oneness back into the collective consciousness. It is our responsibility as their caregivers to assist them in their goals, and honor who they are and what they have come to do. The Crystalline Children carry within them conscious recollection of the wisdom of the ages, and they offer it freely to us.

What will we do? Will we hear their messages and apply the wisdom of the ages to our current lives, our environment, and our world? Or will we choose to remain ignorant, closing door after door within our children along the way? Our children are our future. The future within our kids has the potential to take us to a great turn for the greater good of humanity—if only we will listen to what the children have come to tell us!

Let us honor them and nurture them, and allow ourselves to be open to the possibility that sometimes the children know more than we do. Let us not constrain the possibilities of greater reality just because we don't understand. Instead, let us be open to exploring these amazing gifts with our children. There is no reason to fear them! Gifted as they are, they *are* our children, and their messages are nothing new—just amazing things that most of us have forgotten.

CHECKLIST *for* RECOGNIZING CRYSTALLINE CHILDREN

CHAPTER 5

- ✦ Have eyes of crystal blue or a very deep dark color. They will look at us as if we have known them forever—we have!

- ✦ Have great sensitivity to the environment, the planet, and the feelings of others.

- ✦ Are extremely intuitive.

- ✦ Are generally telepathic.

- ✦ Are socially conscious.

- ✦ Have an innate command of subtle energy.

- ✦ Think compartmentally.

- ✦ Appear very scattered in their attention.

- ✦ Are extremely compassionate.

- ✦ Cannot abide conflict of any kind—they take it personally.

- ✦ Are wise beyond their years.

+ Are peacemakers.

+ Have natural healing abilities.

+ Were born between 1997 and the present (some are a bit older).

+ Are extremely fragile—often become sick with unidentifiable illnesses.

+ Have sweeping energy fields of deep jewel tones or light pastel spectrums.

+ Often remember past lives or their experiences between lives.

+ See and often interact with etheric beings such as angels, Masters, ETs, and so on—will often talk about "visitors" and invisible friends on a very personal level.

+ Some are diagnosed with ADD, ADHD, or autism.

+ Have awareness of their life purpose.

+ Are extremely generous.

+ Are loving, compassionate, and very forgiving.

+ Are aware of interactive dynamics between people.

+ Have an ability to ferret out the truth effortlessly.

+ Need time alone to regenerate or shake off the energies of their day.

+ Are deeply vulnerable yet powerful.

+ Cannot grasp the human ability to be inhumane to others.

+ Have a deep love for life, other people, and animals.

+ Need to experience nature on a regular basis.

+ Love to play or sit in water.

✦ "Magic" happens around them—people become well, money appears, and things change for the better.

✦ Feel responsible for outside events or the actions of others.

✦ Are people magnets—others are attracted to them naturally.

✦ Electronics are often affected by their presence.

✦ Are empathic.

CHILDREN *of the* STARS

CHAPTER 6

The Children of the Stars are a distinct group of children with very special gifts. Parts of their genetic structure have reawakened, bringing to this world aid of interstellar origin. In the future these kids will share new technologies and understanding of the sciences that to date we have only begun to grasp. A Star Child may be defined as a child of both human and extraterrestrial origin. There are many possible reasons for the extraterrestrial contribution to a child's makeup. It may come from reproduction, genetic engineering (intentional blending of multiple races), biomedical technology, telepathic consciousness linking (a "piggy-backing" of one consciousnesses onto another), or even from an intentionally orchestrated incarnation of a Star

Visitor into a human body. Star Visitors include some of the children who have parallel aspects, which we will discuss in a later chapter.

Gaps in archeological evidence suggest that, during certain periods in human evolution, we made great leaps in technology, metallurgy, alchemy, and architectural accomplishments—even transiting between worlds of consciousness that are not understood even now. In human history and evolution there are great gaps in the archeological continuum. In other words, there are large pieces of evidence missing that show a distinct pattern to our physical development.

Most of the artifacts that have ever been unearthed by archeologists demonstrate that the human race seemed to go from being monkey-like to what we are today practically overnight (in evolutionary terms). There appear to be steps missing in our development. For example, in ancient Egyptian tombs, there is evidence of energy manipulation written on the walls. In these pictures, you can see figure after figure carrying balls of white light, orbs of red energy, or inventions that appear to be some type of electrical conduit similar to our contemporary batteries. There are also references of this kind in ancient texts. In the Sumerian "tablets of races" there are references to the Annunaki race—said to come from a distant 10th planet in our solar system. Likewise, in Genesis, the first chapter of the Bible, there are references to the giants that fell from the sky, breeding with humans and creating a whole new race of gifted people. In fact, there are numerous references in ancient literature that suggest we have never been alone in the universe, and that we have, in fact, been influenced by visitors from other times and other places.

Throughout history, art has also depicted Star Visitors. Numerous paintings with religious themes have flying disks in the background or depict flying machines, with some even including otherworldly pilots. In ancient India, these flying machines were called "vishnya," and stories abound of those who traveled in them regularly around Earth and beyond. The gaps in archeological discovery, the objects depicted in historic art, and the sacred words written long ago all suggest that perhaps there were occasions when visitors from other locales in the universe came to our Earth and contributed their genetic materials to us, either by directly breeding with evolving humans or intentionally blending their DNA with our developing biological systems.

In our world today, there are numerous adults who carry within them some of those ancient genetic materials. Their DNA has awakened in new ways, bringing forth new sets of sensibilities. The adults who carry these genetic traits feel as if they have never fit in our world as normal human beings and thus feel a great need to "go home." Many are intuitively or psychically gifted, or exhibit other special talents, such as the inherent ability for remote viewing, healing, and general "knowing" beyond their experiences. These people have commonly been referred to as "Starseeds." Starseeds also have a fascination with certain stars and constellations, particularly Orion, the Pleiades, Arcturas, and Sirius. Some have a particular fascination with Sirius B, which revolves in tandem with Sirius. Some of the Starseeds have brought forth languages, art, literature, music, and symbols that represent their interstellar origin. Starseeds are the forerunners to our Star Children, who are even more genetically and evolutionally progressed. As the DNA of interstellar origin continues to evolve naturally, the Star Children are coming into our world.

The energy fields of Star Children are very finely tuned, and have a completely different set of harmonic energy relationships from those of other human beings. Their energy fields feel smooth and silky, with no static. These fields are rivers of light frequencies that flow uninterrupted—educating, soothing, and replenishing the children as they do so. The Star Kids come to our world with brilliant intelligence. They have a proclivity for, and a grasp of, the sciences and scientific principals that are often difficult for "normal" adults to comprehend. They love to talk about quantum reality.

The Star Children often dream of flying and of rooms filled with white light, or light that is filled with color. They dream of rising into ships and conversing with otherworldly beings. Many of the Star Kids also have a unique effect on electronic equipment, causing it to malfunction or turn off and on randomly. Some Star Children cause street lamps to turn off as they walk down the street or drive by in a car. They have great intuitive gifts and often a full grasp of energy healing. Many of them can see auras and other energy fields. Using their psychic gifts, they can accurately diagnose illness within the physical body. They can also influence others telepathically, and are often clairvoyant. Some have been known to levitate (float above the ground at will) or demonstrate telekinesis (move objects with the mind).

Theses amazing kids are similar to the Crystalline Children in that they think compartmentally. They are able to make astounding leaps in logic, going from hypothesis to solution almost instantaneously. They have an amazing ability to process large amounts of information at once. They seem to receive "downloads" of information, and are able to discuss many different subjects without any evidence whatsoever of ever having studied those subjects in school or anywhere else. Some Star Kids are known to disappear and reappear elsewhere, which can be quite frustrating for parents!

Star Kids are often multidimensionally aware as well. It is easy for them to traverse multiple realities simultaneously and to even discuss those realities with others. It is effortless for them to process information about multiple subjects at once without confusion. They are also able to expand and collapse time consciously—they can actually make events longer or shorter by working outside of time intentionally. They have intrinsic understanding that consciousness is faster than the speed of light, and they use their consciousness to warp time relations as they wish. Star Children are also acutely aware of their environments, and are actively interested in the condition of the planet.

Physically speaking, Star Children often have heads that are somewhat larger than usual. Because of this trait, cesarean sections are often required when they are born. Their body temperature also runs consistently low. For example, instead of the normal basal body temperature of 98.6° F, the Star Kids often have a lower body temperature of 96.8° F, which indicates that their body energy is consumed less rapidly on metabolic levels. The Star Children generally have strong immune systems, and remain particularly healthy under normal circumstances. Unfortunately, because many of the Star Kids are not recognized in their giftedness, some of them become depressed and/or manifest physical illness as a sign of their discomfort.

TREVOR

Trevor was one of the first of the Star Children with whom I worked. Trevor had not only the Star Child energy system, but a broad Crystalline energy field. He also fit the category that I call the Beautiful Silent Ones. At the time that I was working with him, I hadn't yet learned the distinctive differences between the children (or that those differences could combine to create unique situations). Further experience over the years has shown me that this is typical of the fast-forward evolution we are now experiencing. Many of the children do not fit neatly into one category or another. However, primary traits within particular groups do exist.

Trevor's family was particularly supportive because their son exhibited a brilliant combination of gifts. Trevor's mom and dad are some of the front-runners of humanity who instinctively knew to try alternative things to help their son. When I worked with Trevor, he was 9 years old. He was definitely communicating multidimensionally. Trevor did not begin to speak verbally until he was 3 or so, and even then it was in very fragmented sentences. Even at 9 he had difficulty with his speech. He had communicated telepathically from the time he was an infant. At the time, his mom didn't realize what was happening, but she soon caught on! Because of his telepathy, and because his parents always saw him as spiritually evolved, Trevor never needed to speak verbally. His parents have encouraged him to speak only so that he could function on the earthly plane. As Trevor was growing up, quite a few people tried to convince Trevor's mom and dad that he was autistic. Neither parent bought into that, as they knew that their child's differences weren't due to autism.

Trevor often talked about life on another planet where everything was much more comfortable. He said that when he lived there, people looked like "God energy and light." He went on to say that people flew around all of the time, and that they were gentle and loving beings. Trevor told his parents that his earthly body was too uncomfortable and difficult to be in because it was very restrictive. He couldn't wait to fly again and often dreamt of it. Trevor's parents regularly did much to help him be more comfortable in his body. They worked with shamans, who taught them how to journey consciously. ("Journeying" consists of sending your consciousness out of your body, sometimes with a certain intent or question.) The shamanic pathways are vast and varied on many planes of reality and Trevor and his parents have learned to explore the universe together. They love doing so!

Trevor's family has approached his differences from a holistic perspective. They have worked with alternative healers and others as a family so that they can be in tune with each other and support each other in whatever comes up. When Trevor was 15 months old and still could not crawl, his parents took him to a non-force chiropractor. After the first visit, he was crawling and walking on his own. They also worked with a very progressive neurological chiropractor who used kinesiology. As with many families, Trevor's parents ask him about every practitioner before using them. They want Trevor to be comfortable and to be able to participate in the work. This is a vital point. (You may remember William from Chapter 3. William calls out to practitioners prior to steering his mom in their direction, and he also sends his friends when he knows they are ready for certain types of work. This seems to be a status quo with these very gifted children. They are light years ahead of those of us who were not born with such gifts!)

Trevor's parents did various exercises with him, such as Brain Gym. They did their best to find fun ways to integrate work that would help Trevor to learn new physical skills and become stronger. They did the exercises two or three times a week so that it wouldn't become too tedious. Trevor and his family also did yoga together, and he took horseback riding lessons, which he loved. He hasn't become a competing equestrian, but he takes his time and enjoys every minute of it.

Trevor told his family about many of his past lives, most of which were extremely traumatic. When he shared his stories, it was as if he was reliving them at that moment. As he spoke of the details, the depth of his feeling was extreme, as if his soul ached from the memories. Similar to some of the other children described in this book, Trevor had several night visitors who were not always friendly. They seem to be people who had just died—as if Trevor was some type of conduit between this world and the spirit world. Trevor said that first he saw the deceased person and then angels arrived to escort him or her to the spirit world. When Trevor's parents asked him what the spirits wanted from him, all he told them was that apparently the spirits needed comforting and reassurance before they went on. His parents have taught him how to protect himself by using Source light, and they have told him about deciding which beings are acceptable to him. That has worked very well for him.

Trevor also told his parents that right before he came to the Earth plane, Jesus told him to be very careful of his body. His spirit guides chose his parents because they knew that they would take great care of Trevor. (Time after time this writer has heard story after story about children informing their parents about why they were chosen. This seems to be a common thread amongst the Children of Now.)

One summer, Trevor told his parents about a dog who had gone into their yard at night. He said that he "flew" downstairs and went outside to be with the dog. The dog was dying and in great pain, so Trevor asked the dog if he could put his hand into his body to help him. The dog answered yes ("in his mind," as Trevor calls it). Trevor put his hand in the dog's body, and the dog thanked him for taking his pain away. Then angels came and took the dog back to the spirit world. This was Trevor's first excursion with a canine, but his nights are often filled with flying and otherworldly experiences.

Trevor's parents expressed what so many others in their position have—namely, that they have felt very isolated in their experiences with their very special child. After all, talking about their strange experiences with others sometimes leads to ostracism or worse. Parents in these situations crave others with whom they can share their experiences. I haven't talked with Trevor's family for several years. The last I heard, Trevor still had extreme emotional swings and was occasionally battling the fear for his body and some of what he was able to see—in particular, some of the beings who are curious about him—although he has become more "present" with others than he had been previously. I say, hats off to Trevor's mom and dad! They are a perfect example of parents who are flexible and creative, and who truly pay attention to the extraordinary needs of their child.

JOHN EVERETT

Certain places that I have visited over the years have greatly enriched and developed my practice. Usually when I revisit those locations, my schedule is full to capacity and I have a waiting list. There are some who come regularly, and others who come whom I have never met. One evening on such an occasion, it was time for my last appointment of the day. I knew a little bit about the situation ahead of time from the person who had booked the appointment for me. Apparently I was to work with a boy who was about 7 years old. John Everett and his mom, Francis, came on time for the appointment. Francis was a little bit nervous, not really knowing what to expect. John Everett was dressed in red pajamas. He was small and slight of build for his age, and his silky smooth complexion gave his little face the impression of perfection. He had medium brown hair and a slight air of defeat. I wondered why.

A vision in red, John Everett carried a book that was almost as big as he was. The book was about military aircraft and was about 2 inches thick, the type one might see on a coffee table. He carried it quite possessively and did not put it down when he sat on the couch. Francis was quite chatty, talking about Indigo Children and a book about them she had read. Someone had told her that John Everett was an Indigo, and Francis had made sure that the principal and staff of John Everett's school all had a personal copy of that Indigo book so that they could learn about the gifted children (go mom!). Francis was concerned because John Everett's performance in school was not adequate for his obvious intelligence, and she was absolutely sure something must be wrong with him. From what I could gather, she seemed to have a desire for her son to become an overachiever. Francis meant well, but to me, it was obvious that she was exerting too much pressure on her child—or, at least that was what I initially thought.

John Everett wasn't particularly interested in talking with me at first because he didn't know me. Early in our session I observed that Francis would ask John Everett a question and then answer it for him. He seemed a bit exasperated with that, and I have to admit that his exasperation with her was a bit contagious! John Everett had little need to say much. To establish a rapport with him, I showed an interest in his airplane book. I told him that my dad was in the Air Force and that I couldn't remember which plane he flew. John Everett lit up like a Christmas tree. He opened the book to exactly the correct page and began a litany of the features of the plane my dad had flown. Then he launched into a comparison between that plane and others that came before and after it. It was amazing. John Everett knew every detail about every plane—from structure, hydraulics, and mechanics, to problems with and strengths of the crafts. It was as if he was a walking encyclopedia of airplanes. But that was just the beginning.

I turned the conversation from airplanes to school, asking him about his experiences there. I quickly realized that John Everett wasn't particularly interested in the subject, and so I asked him why. Instead of answering me directly, John Everett turned to his mother and said, "Mom, if you had to take a test about everything that happened every day since you were born, could you answer those questions? Would you care? After all, you have lived a whole life since then!" Francis looked a bit puzzled, and it took a moment for what he was really saying to hit home. About the time I got it John Everett continued:

"Look, in school the teachers tell us to read things, they teach us things. After that, I learn a lot more than they can tell me; it is as if I live lifetimes during each week. Then the teachers expect me to go backwards to remember all of those little details that no longer matter because I am light years ahead of them. Of course I rush through them. To me, those tests are meaningless, a waste of time! I already know all that stuff!"

Hmmm. I was beginning to realize that this child was more of a prodigy than anyone realized. Maybe Mom was right! I engaged John Everett in conversation about what he was learning that was so much more important than his school work. As we talked, John Everett decided to get on the healing table and allow me to work with him. As I accessed his field, it was clear to me that this child was a fine-tuned masterpiece and that there was little work to be done. His energy field hummed at a very high frequency with almost no variation. It was clear and intense. It is not unusual for Star Children to exhibit some traits of Crystalline energy within their energy fields, and John Everett was no exception.

As I worked, John Everett and I talked and our conversation began to turn toward some amazing subject matter. Before long, we were discussing multidimensional reality, black holes, parallel realities, parallel universes, harmonic relationships, worm holes, and more—all described in the kind of fine detail that only one who has experienced those realities could understand. His amazing breadth of knowledge was staggering even for me. His confidence and ease with each subject exuded from every pore. I quickly realized that John Everett was simply bored. He had no one with whom he could relate. No one could converse with him about much of his reality, so he stayed quiet, let his mom do most of the talking, and quietly went on with his learning process and multidimensional journeys. I was excited beyond words.

John Everett was obviously a Child of the Stars, and I was captivated. It is not often that another person can talk with me about the same kinds of unusual experiences I have had. We were like two peas in a pod, both of us excited that the other could keep up with the conversation. I talked with Francis, explaining to her that John Everett simply needed to be heard by people who could understand him—even if that meant arranging for him to sit in on college club meetings and classes, astronomy classes, or whatever would interest him. John Everett has the capacity for processing incredible amounts and combinations and amounts of data simultaneously, and his interests grow exponentially. I suggested that Francis work more to socialize John Everett in arenas that would be mutually beneficial for John Everett and his acquaintances, as well as feed his insatiable desire to learn new things. Most of John Everett's interests were in the sciences, so I gave Francis some suggestions about organizations she could contact.

When I told her frankly that there was nothing wrong with her son, Francis almost seemed surprised. This was mostly because she was completely unable to relate to John Everett's great stretches of intelligence. Having such a child can be a challenge! When such children are misunderstood, there is a lack of encouragement for the children's giftedness, and they are sometimes seen instead as defective. The attention they are given is not nurturing and encouraging; rather, it is directed toward the labeled dysfunction. The child's identity becomes the label or diagnosis, and when that occurs, the child stagnates in a pool of societal waste. Somehow I felt that if I could better explain John Everett's differences, then they might be easier for his mom to grasp. Not knowing her prior to that session, I was careful not to frighten her by stretching her reality too far at once. I feel that labeling anyone defines them so that the possibilities of expansion are lost, so I was unwilling to provide a specific label for her son. I carefully and thoughtfully explained to Francis about the Children of Now, and spoke to her of her son's skills and the reasons for them. As we talked, Francis became more relaxed and began to understand that John Everett was not malfunctioning at all; in fact, he was *hyperfunctioning*. No one knew to ask him just how far he had gone with his learning because his abilities didn't fit into the normal societal structure. He was being accused of being lazy, when in fact he was running circles around the intelligence of those around him.

I recently had the chance to visit with John Everett, and he is growing into a fine-looking young man, with eyes that, as you look into them, take you to infinite places. He is working on some pretty neat inventions and continues to thrive. When Francis took him out of the public school, he began to make huge strides in his studies because he was no longer being held back. Francis is doing a fantastic job, not only in catching on to John Everett's needs, but in supporting herself during the process.

John Everett is only one of many children like this whom I have encountered. They are so brilliant that few can relate to them. Some of them spend so much time isolated in their awareness that they become lost within their brilliance. And they have so much to share!

STEVEN

Our DNA—the genetic materials that determine what we look like and even what we are capable of—is filled with information from, and memories of, everything that came before us. That information is further translated into cellular memory. Our cellular memory carries ancestral information that propagates family behavioral patterns. The information carried within our DNA, and consequently our cellular materials, is communicated to our earthly experience. Some people actually have cognitive memories about past lives. Others have physical afflictions or pains that have no apparent cause but are very real in the here and now. Past-life memories that are stored in our bodies are very real, as are the symptoms that those memories cause. Because of this, the Star Children often suffer from strange afflictions that the medical community has difficulty diagnosing, if they can find answers at all. Their bodies carry memories of previous conflict or injury as easily as they bring forth mental brilliance. The children may exhibit pain, fevers, malaise, depression, organ dysfunction, or other anomalous symptoms. One such child is one whom I will call Steven.

Steven's mom brought him to me because he had ongoing health issues. Steven seemed to be declining and depression had set in. He had headaches that were extremely painful, and a general malaise that he seemed unable to escape. Like John Everett, he was so highly intelligent that others could not easily relate to him, if at all. He felt set aside from others in his family, from his few friends, and from the kids at school. Recognizing his extreme intelligence, Steven's dad pushed him very hard, demanding perfection from him. It was a lot of pressure for a little guy. As I talked with Steven's mom, I came to the conclusion that the entire family was involved. Mom in particular was intuitively gifted, and she and all of Steven's siblings had strange and severe medical issues. I began to understand that we were working with a family that shared the traits of Starseed and consecutive generation Star Children.

As I began working with Steven, I noticed that his energy field felt as if it were being drained, and I searched for the cause. For a while I was unable to see or feel the reason for what I sensed. As I worked through Steven's energy layers, one after the other was out of the ordinary. His energy fields were out of harmony, and there were strange looking blockages everywhere. The blockages seemed to restrict some of the communication within Steven's energy field, and the communication was of a pattern that I did not recognize. Moving through one layer at a time, I commanded repairs, and the energy field began to harmonize. The blockages were removed and energy began to flow more normally.

As I worked at Steven's head, I was guided to work on his ears. On the left ear there was a bulge in the middle of the ear tissue. According to Chinese acupuncture charts, this particular area of the ear has to do with the pituitary gland, the thyroid, and the brain, all of which regulate the body in different ways. I had a sense that the bulge may be an implant of some kind because of the way it felt. Usually when we work with acupressure points, energy is released. In this instance, the area of the ear actually *drew* energy when I worked on it. The area felt foreign in relation to the balance of Steven's energy field and his physical body, and the mass did not diminish when I worked on it. I knew that this was the source of Steven's headaches. Whatever this thing was, it was out of harmony with the rest of him and it was causing him physical pain. I worked on the area some more, made some changes to it harmonically, and instructed mom how to do more of the same at home. I still did not feel that I had found everything that was causing Steven's problems, so I kept looking. Finally I found it.

Each of us has a field of energy that surrounds us completely. It is similar to a warm cocoon that acts as a barrier and an interpreter between us and all of creation. This field "steps down" incoming messages so that our consciousness can translate what it receives into actual cognition. Similarly, what we experience, think, and feel is translated outwardly as refined energy into all of creation. In a way, our surrounding field also holds us together as manifested beings. All of the tiny particles that comprise us come together in harmonic arrangements that are snuggled safely within our surrounding field. Part of this field can be seen by some people in the form of auras. The size of our exterior field depends on our harmonic resonance within creation, as well as on our physical, spiritual, emotional, and spiritual states. When we do not feel well, our surrounding field becomes smaller, and stays closer to our bodies to preserve energy. When we feel fantastic and are in our "heart space," our field becomes huge, communicating more easily to our surroundings.

Steven's field exhibited a strange anomaly. At the very top of his field, directly over his heart area, there was an unusual, scarred-looking attachment. The attachment was parasitic, and it was draining Steven's vitality. Frankly I had never seen anything like that. When working on an energy system multidimensionally, we are technically accessing the entire history of that person in all of their lifetimes. This particular attachment was of ancient, intergalactic origin. It was much like the pilot fish that hitches rides with whales or sharks. However, pilot fish are generally symbiotic with the whales and sharks because they perform a service for their hosts by cleaning their bodies as they eat. In Steven's case, the attachment wasn't serving him. In fact, it was robbing him of vital life force. The afflicted area of Steven's field had thickened, restricting the fluidity of the energy. There was also a dark region in the center of the thickened area, and there seemed to be an unusual energy present there—a life force that was different from Steven's own sweet energy.

I did not immediately know what to do with this situation, and was candid with Steven's mom about my puzzlement. (Interdimensional healing work is very different from other kinds of healing. Each person has a history all his or her own, so every session is different and a learning process in its own right.) I told Steven's mom that I needed some time to sort out all of the information I was receiving and to make sense of what I saw. I worked with Steven for several weeks, watching the attachment and allowing myself to feel what was going on. Ultimately, I was able to vanquish the attachment. Upon making the repair, Steven made a remarkable recovery. His headaches disappeared and his energy level normalized. Other problems he had also went away. Amazing.

I have noticed that many of the Star Kids who are having problems generally have anomalous attachments and or blockages within their energy systems. Of course, not all of the Star Kids have these, but if they are suffering from unidentified maladies, it is likely that there is a need to look at different parts of the anatomy—the etheric aspects!

CRAIG

Other Star Kids are very in tune with extraterrestrials, or visitors from other worlds. On the way to present at a conference, arrangements were made for me to be picked up at the airport by the daughter of one of the other presenters. When she met me at the airport, she had her son with her. I will call him Craig. He was in a child safety seat in the backseat. Craig was a slightly built, dark-haired 6-year-old, with great big brown eyes that betrayed his hyperalertness and intelligence. He was intimidated by me at first because his mom introduced me to him as "Dr. Meg." I realized that he had mistaken me for a medical doctor, and that had definitely intimidated him!

The drive was about an hour and a half, and during our trip Craig eventually loosened up and began to tell me about certain dreams that he had. To me, his dreams sounded just like descriptions of classic alien abduction experiences. He was highly aware of other presences— even as we rode in the car, Craig told us that "they" were flying in the sky as we talked. Craig's mom looked up and around and said that she couldn't see anything. Craig's response was honest-to-God impatience that "she wasn't looking fast enough!" In that moment I realized that Craig was using his etheric sight and was actually seeing multidimensionally. As I tuned in with him, I could see them too. "They" were definitely "out there."

The Star Children are wondrous beings. They are not only intellectually and psychically gifted, but they also recognize the importance of their spiritual connection to the Source, and to all other creation as well. They share common spiritual insights, and enjoy exploring the connections between the physical, metaphysical, and spiritual aspects of being. Star Kids are often overwhelmed with an inherent need to help people awaken to their highest and best potential. Star Kids also want to change the world for the better. They strive to instill peace through their compassion and kind deeds. They work to heal the Earth and can feel the planetary energies. When anyone is willing to listen, they delight in telling us about our family among the stars. The Star Kids have intelligence and universal understanding that will ultimately bring new and exciting technologies to our world. Those technologies will be symbiotic with our planet, and will contribute to great strides in the pursuit of comfort for all of humanity.

The Star Children are not a curiosity, just a normal part of our evolutionary process. They are the front-runners of other, even more intellectually advanced beings. We must give these children whatever it takes to feed their great mental capacity. We must give them the nurturing that they need to sustain their fragile bodies. Most of all, we must realize that the strange things of which they speak are not fantasy, but are, in fact, indicative of a greater reality that will someday be a part of our everyday awareness, our technology, and our very lives.

CHECKLIST *for* RECOGNIZING STAR CHILDREN

CHAPTER 7

- ✦ Have high intelligence—often, but not always, gifted in areas of the sciences.
- ✦ Are greatly sensitive to their environment.
- ✦ Have heightened sensitivity to the energies and emotions of others.
- ✦ Are physically smaller than many children their age.
- ✦ Demonstrate enhanced psychic abilities.
- ✦ Have the ability to harness the subtle energy fields found in and around the body (bio-energetics).
- ✦ Are able to use earthly and cosmic forces to heal.
- ✦ Are gifted in telepathic and intuitive communication with others and with Source Consciousness.

+ Often affect electronics or other electrical items, sometimes causing them to malfunction.

+ Can communicate mentally (telepathy).

+ Are able to predict the future (precognition).

+ Can move objects by changing their relationship to reality (telekinesis).

+ Can mentally see things distant in space or time (clairvoyance/remote viewing).

+ Can "download" information from non-local realities.

+ Have penetrating intuitiveness (just "know" things without being told).

+ Able to remotely influence others (telepathically).

+ Can learn about another's health, intentions, motivations, and so on by "reading" the energy field surrounding them.

+ Are able to diagnose illness or malfunction within another's energy fields.

+ Able to perform psychic or bio-energetic healing.

+ Can move self or an object from one locale to another by mental effort (teleportation).

+ Can rise from the ground, defying gravity (levitation).

+ Are able to work outside of time, causing events to occur rapidly (or conversely, slowing them to an extreme).

+ Are sensitive to imminent earthquakes and other disasters.

+ Have multidimensional awareness.

✦ Able to travel "out of body" (astral projection).

✦ Can open their consciousness and allow etheric beings to speak through them (channeling).

✦ Often have a shared consciousness with a Star Visitor guide.

✦ Operate in close mental connection with their Star Nation guides, and can physically summon and connect with these guides and other guardians.

✦ Have strong immune systems (or conversely, strange illnesses with no apparent physical cause).

✦ Have a lower basal body temperature.

✦ Have a dynamic appearance and personality.

✦ Have a commanding presence.

✦ Look younger than their years later in life (as do adult Starseeds).

PARALLEL ASPECTS: CHILDREN of the EARTH and STARS

CHAPTER 8

*I'd rather be back in Atlantis. I was
happy there. I like to go back there because
when I am out of my physical body I am free!
I can run I can fly
I can be anything, anywhere that I want!*
—William, age 11

There are other aspects, or parts of us, that reside on other planes of reality. Similar to the petals of a flower, each of our aspects is a little bit different from the next, but taken together, they create the beautiful, intricate, and infinite whole of who we are in creation. Remove any of those petals and the flower becomes out of balance, lacking. An aspect is also similar to our shadow. Our shadow is always there, but its location and appearance depends on the direction and amount of light that is present at any given time. Our shadow moves in harmony with us, but it is not the same thing as our physical selves. Our shadow may be longer or shorter than we are, and sometimes it is lighter or darker, but it is always there. Similarly, our aspects don't all look the same, but each one is vital to us and to all of our other aspects as well. When our aspects are functional and in proper alignment, they work harmonically with us, but they have a certain distance from us, depending upon the dimension in which they reside.

There is a part of our consciousness that has experiences that are very different from the ones we have in our everyday, third-dimensional lives, and these experiences directly affect who and what we are in our earthly existence. We are made of layers of electromagnetic energy fields that are constructed of fine frequencies—frequencies that have color, sound, and vibration. Taken together, these frequencies are what make us who and what we are. Each set of frequencies creates an aspect, and determines at what level that aspect will vibrate, and the vibration establishes what dimension that aspect will reside in. Normally, no two of our aspects have identical or nearly identical sets of frequencies. Instead, each layer, each aspect, is in perfect harmony with the aspects above and below it.

From a universal perspective, all events—past, present, and future—are occurring at the same time. Parts of us experience past lives, or live in other galaxies or other planes of reality, while other parts of us worry about paying the mortgage or what might happen tomorrow. There are other parts of us who are already living tomorrow!

Figure 6. An example of normal aspect harmonization.

Our multidimensional aspects are formed in the same fashion. Each aspect we have is a harmonized set of frequencies that is a little bit different from each level to the next (see Figure 6). The totality of all of our aspects is who and what we are, energetically and harmonically and in relation to everything else in creation. We are similar to a giant musical chord, with one tone (aspect) after another creating a sound vibration that is ours alone. That combined sound vibration is what makes each of us harmonically unique, to the point that we actually hold space in the fabric of creation. As we harmonize within the context of creation, *we are an integral and contributive part of everything that is.* Our exclusive harmonic makeup dictates how we function, how we look, and where we manifest as beings—whether that is here on Earth, at another time, at another place, or even on another planet. Sometimes our harmonic makeup even dictates what we experience. In a way, each one of us is an entire "soul family" unto ourselves—but I won't go too far into that now because that subject alone would fill another book!

There are many problems that can arise when our aspects are not harmonically aligned. For instance, if an aspect that resides on a plane of reality near the third dimension is out of alignment or out of harmony, we might experience a sense of disconnectedness, feel ungrounded, have trouble concentrating or making decisions, or generally feel very scattered. The effects of the dysfunction depend upon the degree of the misalignment, and the emotions or events that were the root cause (see Figure 7). Likewise, when aspects become too similar harmonically, dysfunction will occur in one or more of our aspects.

Figure 7. An example of fragmentation among the aspects. Note that
there are blank layers where the aspects have moved out of place.
This causes gaps in the energetic communication system.
Other aspects aren't connected at all, such as the one
in the upper right corner.

There are different reasons for aspect imbalance to occur. Sometimes our aspects will have such similar kinds of experiences that their frequencies naturally harmonize at closely related sets of frequencies. When that occurs, all of the aspects of that person typically "re-harmonize" along with the one that has changed. If the experience of re-harmonization is a positive one, the frequencies of all of the aspects will usually rise in vibration, and all levels will function reasonably well together.

At other times, one or more of our aspects may fragment away from our harmonic structure. This often happens during times of great trauma, or in situations in which people are unable to cope with what is happening to them. This could be a result of physical or emotional abuse, or when a person is victimized during a traumatic situation. If there is a lack of coping skills, the victim internalizes his or her feelings into neat little compartments, in which his or her feelings are "locked up" energetically.

The energetic compartments then break away from the main energy system, and no longer cooperate harmonically with the other aspects. When fragmentation occurs, there are gaps in the harmonic organization. This is a lot like a ladder that is missing some of its rungs: In order to climb the ladder you have to step very high to avoid the missing rungs. In these instances our aspects begin to communicate similarly; after a while, the functional aspects begin to leave out the isolated ones, often skipping them entirely. Because part of the "ladder" is inaccessible, full communication is impossible amongst all of the aspects.

When there is fragmentation, the earthly manifestation (us) begins to exhibit symptoms of dysfunction—we become indecisive and unable to focus our attention, and our moods swing without warning. Sometimes our physical energy does too. We feel stuck, as if there is no forward motion in our lives, and perhaps we even feel lost, as if we do not have a road map to guide us through our life.

When we are fragmented, the fact is that some of our road map really *is* missing. The only way to repair that is to find the missing or recalcitrant aspects and assimilate them back into harmony with the whole. Ethereally, this looks much like a Russian nesting doll, with one inside the other, then another, and so on. When we assimilate aspects, we are essentially re-harmonizing them into one functional unit. Sometimes this process is referred to as "soul retrieval," as if the missing aspects are fragments of a soul that have broken away.

Parallel aspects occur when two different aspects of the same person become nearly identical harmonically in two different times and places. Parallel aspects are multidimensional, yet they have such similar frequencies that each has conscious awareness of the other. Imagine living two lives at the same time and having awareness of both experiences! It is almost as if there are two people living in one body (see Figure 8). Parallel aspects can contribute much to intellect, conscious memory, intuition, extrasensory perception, and multidimensional awareness. They can also contribute to memories of past lives. And talk about depth of character—a child with parallel aspects is always full of surprises!

Having parallel aspects may also contribute to major physical dysfunction. There is a universal law that clearly dictates that there cannot be two identical sets of frequencies at the same time in creation, so when parallel aspects harmonize too closely, part of the harmonization of one or both of the aspects will break down. This breaking down occurs on a physical level last, because our physicality is denser than any other part of our makeup and therefore the slowest to respond to changes within the energetic system. Which biological systems become affected depend upon where the harmonic duplication occurs.

Figure 8. Parallel aspects—two aspects of self that have harmonized to nearly identical frequencies, causing malfunction in both aspects.

When aspects are parallel, interesting phenomenon occur. Neither of the parallel aspects can exist normally. By universal law, one of the aspects must dominate the other. The aspect that is not usually present in the third dimension resides in a form of consciousness, which is always present and lives vicariously through the third-dimensional body. The third-dimensional body and consciousness are able to freely experience whatever the parallel aspect does. Essentially, there are two sets of consciousness working as one within the person.

I have found that certain subgroups of the Star and Crystalline Children have parallel aspects that are all of intergalactic origin. (All of the children I know who fit this category are about 10 to 12 years old at this writing, with most of them being about 11.) In other words, an aspect that used to live on another planet—often in a parallel universe or another place in time—is so closely harmonized with the earthly self that the two are in conflict. Because it is far more evolved and able to use its consciousness to the point of commanding reality, the intergalactic aspect usually harmonizes to function with the third-dimensional aspect. More often than not it does so for survival purposes.

Children who exhibit parallel aspects generally display major physical disabilities. The type of dysfunction varies, but there are commonalities in the experiences of these children and their families. Nearly all of the children in this category cannot or will not speak. They are highly telepathic and reach across time and space to those whom they know can hear them. Many of these children travel and communicate in the form of orbs. These children also exhibit fantastic gifts of intuitive perception, multidimensional awareness, and telepathy. Some are even capable of teleportation! The positive side to parallel aspects is that, even though they exist in a dysfunctional physical body, these children are able to travel through time and space, so they almost always feel quite free. Also, as I stated before, the parallel aspect brings high intelligence, and a sense of universal connectedness that is rarely seen in most other human beings. These little ones are Masters on Earth.

Repairing a parallel aspect situation requires special care and attention. Parallel aspects cannot simply be assimilated or joined as one, because they would nearly cancel each other out. Instead, a kind of synergy amongst the aspects much be accomplished. To do this, the two aspects must be harmonized together so that they are able to cleanly and smoothly work together, but still remain as individuals. Harmonization looks much like a musical chord that, because of its combination of notes, creates a third set of frequencies called overtones, or implied harmonics. The overtones act as a bridge to close the gap between the two aspects, allowing for communication between them and all other aspects of the child. Synergistic harmonization is very different from assimilation, which occurs when the aspects are simply harmonized as individuals.

There is an entire group of children who have parallel aspects. I call them the Beautiful Silent Ones. Despite the various physical setbacks and disabilities that often come with having parallel aspects, these children are telepathic, intuitive, spiritual Masters who have a lot to share with our world. What is truly amazing is that they are almost all 11 years old now. Gender has no bearing on this phenomenon, as there are boys and girls who have contacted me in various ways. This is always done telepathically, and sometimes by involving their parents as their "voices" to call me on the phone, e-mail me, or introduce the children in person. Usually the parents have not heard of me until the child asks them to contact me!

Each child who has come forward has identified him- or herself as one of the orbs. Imagine, those orbs of consciousness that have joined my energy field all have names, faces, and personalities—in fact, they are very real children and Masters, each in their own right!

OUR BEAUTIFUL SILENT ONES

CHAPTER 9

The hardest part for a parent and for other people as well, is getting past the fact that my child looks broken and the idea that she needs to be fixed. We need to realize that she is an amazingly gifted being just as she is... she exudes nothing but pure love.
—Karen, mother of Lorrin

When the children first began to contact me in orb form, I thought that my imagination was getting the best of me! But, as they have contacted me directly one by one via telepathy, through their parents, or by personal appearances, I have come to realize that this phenomenon is indisputably real.

Within the group of children who communicate telepathically, there is a small group that I have deemed the Beautiful Silent Ones.

They are amazing children who, at a glance, appear to be considerably less than perfect, in fact nonfunctional—at least on the outside. But on the inside these kids carry beauty that is often overwhelming in its message, and heart-expanding in its truth. Our Beautiful Silent Ones may be Crystalline or Children of the Stars; they may be combinations of many of the different evolutionary energetic patterns. Then again, perhaps not. I have come to the conclusion that these particular children are the forerunners of the new evolution of humanity. They have moved into nearly pure conscious existence while remaining present in our physical world, albeit with apparent dysfunction. Their wisdom and purity of heart exceeds general human perception. They speak as if God is talking through them, and they are interpreting his words for the world.

We are generally socialized to think that people who are differently able should be avoided. We turn away from them in horror because we don't want to catch something they might have. We look the other way so as to not be embarrassed.

Start looking.

Just because a person is in a body that doesn't work well doesn't mean that his or her consciousness isn't vital and aware. If you were ever to encounter children like the ones in this book, you would never look at an apparently disabled person the same way again. We have to pay attention!

Our Silent Children are amazing. They do not appear to know or be capable of much, but once we get past the outside appearances, what we find are fully functional beings who have a lot to offer our world. Their conscious-ness roams freely beyond their physical bodies through all of reality. They travel to other times and places, and with a sense of humor that never ceases to amaze. They communicate telepathically and with ease. People who have been around these kids will attest to some wondrous happenings, as we will see later on. They teach absolute and pure love simply by being. And they ask for nothing in return. While they may seem to be nothing but challenges to their families and caregivers, these silent ones are great gifts to our world. The Beautiful Silent Ones are physically affected for different reasons: genetic mutation, head or brain injuries, reactions to vaccines, or congenital problems, to name a few. Although each child is decidedly different in why they are the way they are, this magnificent group of kids share some amazing traits.

MORE ABOUT WILLIAM

Earlier I promised to talk more about William. He was the first of the children who was projecting orb consciousness to communicate with me and who showed up as a very real human child. When I first began working with William I knew that something strange was going on. When I looked at his etheric energy fields, I saw two of him. William had been seeing a gifted healer for some time, and she had discovered the same thing. She called the duplicate William his twin flame. (A twin flame is another being that comes from exactly the same original energy expression. Usually they come in the form of a perfect mate, where two people together actually feel as if they make a whole. This is the perfect love!) I have never seen or considered a twin flame to be a duplicate of a person, so as I watched and waited for instructions, the information I received was that this was a parallel aspect. That parallel aspect was of intergalactic nature. In other words, another part of William existed who lived in another time on another planet. Yes, this is very strange, but true nonetheless. (It's important to note here that not every one of the

Beautiful Silent Ones has a parallel aspect. I don't want everyone to think that just because a child has physical limitations means that they are out of multidimensional alignment.) William was the first of several who exhibited this phenomenon. In time, and with William's, help we were able to repair this phenomenon by creating a harmonic bridge that allowed both aspects to function individually yet harmonically with each other, so that neither interfered with the other. William has been improving steadily ever since.

William is one of the Beautiful Silent Ones. Eleven years old at this writing, he doesn't speak, and he has spatial and coordination issues due to his physical limitations. He is, however, a brilliant child. He is being homeschooled, and he is already surpassing his mom in math. She is wondering how she will keep up with him as he progresses! William and I have worked together on many occasions, and, amazingly, his energy field is evolving at warp speed. When I first began to work with him, William's field was typical Crystalline, with deep jewel tones of all the colors of the rainbow. Because of his parallel aspect, the field had interference in it, causing the patterns of energy movement to sweep in an irregular fashion. Each time we come together for a session, I find that William's energy field has become more and more refined. At this writing, his energy field is so smooth, so perfect, that he is in tune with everything and everyone.

Some of these children are so extremely sensitive that they develop idiosyncrasies that may seem odd, but are extremely necessary for their comfort and, at times, even for their survival. William is so sensitive that he cannot stand wearing shoes or even clothing most of the time. This can be a bit exasperating for his family and visitors to their home! He has lately been acclimating to clothing, but he absolutely cannot go the extra mile and wear shoes. This is because the energy force that moves through his body is so strong that it can be physically uncomfortable as it exits through his feet. If he wears shoes, his feet will actually heat up and he will feel imbalanced. When William can feel the earth under his feet, it is easier for him to remain consciously present in our world. William's mom maintains a sense of humor about his oddities. William is well-known to turn off street lights as he walks under them, and create other electrical anomalies, such as power failures in buildings. While she is sometimes understandably exasperated with him, William's mom has learned to find great humor in his strangeness, and is completely and wonderfully supportive of him.

As we have since he first showed up to me as an orb form, William and I communicate telepathically on a regular basis between our sessions. He pops into my head at the most unexpected times, and sometimes this can yield humorous results. Recently I was in a recording studio in New York City, working on a new guided meditation CD for children to help them let go of their problems, worries, and fears, and to find their positive feelings so that they can share them outwardly. The meditation takes the children on an inward journey of discovery that has them opening little boxes, each with its specific content.

As I was recording a particular part, I encouraged the children to fill their "imagination box" with whatever they wanted (this box is empty, because imagination is unlimited). Because I am an extremely visual person, I was literally seeing and experiencing what I was asking the children to do. Suddenly, and with a familiar feeling, my reality shifted, and all of a sudden the box in my vision filled with bullfrogs that began to spill out all over the place and hop away. I knew that William had once again invaded my reality. I began to laugh as I realized what was happening. I actually left that part on the CD because it made it more fun for the listener.

When he feels that he is ready for more healing work, William contacts me telepathically. His mom is often a bit disconcerted when she e-mails me to schedule an appointment and I have already done it. But she is a great sport, and needless to say we do laugh a lot. Because all of our sessions are long-distance, when I work with William I ask him to participate with me ethereally. This is possible because he is multidimensionally gifted. When he assists, William's sessions show great results. There is also a greatly humorous side to working with him. Recently, as I was getting close to the end of a healing session with William, my "connection" was cut off and my mind filled with pictures—little movies of clowns. Lots of them! He had the clowns making faces at me and doing silly things. I burst out laughing. Apparently William had determined that we had accomplished what we set out to do. Telepathically I replied that I knew we were done. Okay, okay, I get it, William!

Another time, as we finished a session, my reality shifted and I saw an entire crew of odd-looking people who appeared to be on board a spaceship that looked not unlike the bridge of the Starship Enterprise on *Star Trek*. The one I was seeing in my mind was a bit more worn. There was a very tall male who seemed to be in charge. When I called William's mom after the session, I asked her if he had a particular interest in Star Trek movies. What she told me was amazing. She said "Oh, you mean the really tall guy? That is William's best friend, Ooloo. He has visited my sister with Ooloo lots of times."

William often visits his aunt in the same way he visits me. He also contacts people he would like to work with or meet and lets them know he is coming. His telepathy is not at all limited to me, and grows continually as the web of people who can hear him continues to expand. William also refers other children to me. He tells them when they arc ready for the work that I do. His guidance of the other kids has a lot to do with the state of evolution of their energy fields. If they are not yet refined enough, William will tell them to hold off. When they get to a certain evolutionary state, he passes these children on to me.

On a more serious side, as part of his healing, William and I have taken "trips" together into his past, and even into the lives of some of his other aspects. There are reasons for this. As we live our lives, and have lived other lives before this one, we constantly exchange energy with other people, places, and even events. Each time we move into a new life experience, we carry what we have been and done up to that point. Sometimes some of that energy is dysfunctional or damaged. William decided that he needed to go back to Atlantis. He gave no explanation as to why; he just said that it was important. He asked his mom to arrange for me to help him go back there. At the agreed time, we did just that. William was quite familiar with the layout of Atlantis, and took me to sites there that I had never seen in my own journeys of consciousness. It soon became apparent to me that William had ended his life there with some unfinished business, which he completed on our excursion. It was a powerful and emotional moment as he completed the task he had waited lifetimes to finish.

During that particular expedition, after we had accomplished our main goal, we had the chance to play for a while. We found ourselves in a field by a river, with wildflowers blooming everywhere. It felt like early spring. William began to run across the field (which was a beautiful thing, as even walking in this world is a great challenge for him!). He was gleeful, teasing me about keeping up, and reminding me that there was no reason I couldn't because I wasn't in my body! We came to a little house at the far end of the field. The next thing I knew we were inside in a small room. William was looking down with an expression of pure reverence and love in his eyes. As I followed his gaze, I saw a woman holding a baby. I was touched beyond words as William introduced me to his twin flame, his eternal love who, in that place and time, had just been born. She was a gorgeous baby girl with Crystalline blue eyes, which were dreamily alert and seemed to hold the wisdom of all time. William touched her tiny little hand very gently, and I could see that his entire heart energy was literally reaching into hers with love. Of course I cried. It was beyond beautiful. Imagine being able to find your forever love anytime, and in another time and place!

"Out there," William's disabilities do not exist. He is fully able and very excited to be free of his restrictive and malfunctioned physical body. Playing ethereally with William is fun. The fact that we travel in this way is particularly amazing, because he lives in California and I currently live in Tennessee! We can hear each other as if we were in the same room. We have taken several journeys together, and it never ceases to amaze me that all of this is even possible. But it is, and with practice it becomes easier.

Other children have come forward in the same fashion. To me, this has been a mind-bending experience. When it first began, I definitely questioned my perceptions. Most sane people don't go around communicating with invisible orbs and connecting them to real people! But it is all very real, and it is still happening. William was only the first. It wasn't some fluke of imagination or temporary insanity— quite the contrary. The orbs continue to come forward and communicate, and as time moves on I realize that more and more of them have faces, names, and families. Each day is an amazing ride, and there have been enough validations, enough parents and others involved, who have corroborated my experiences that there can be no question as to the reality of these communications. Some of the parents told me that they had never heard of me before their child instigated the contact between us. We all quickly find out why!

LORRIN

At one time I was in Scottsdale, Arizona, for the Celebrate Your Life conference. I was talking with someone I knew and had my back to the room. All of a sudden, much as it was with William, my awareness completely changed gears and I lost track of the conversation completely. At the same time I heard the words, "Hi, I made it!" There were about 2,000 people there, but I had a pretty good idea of what I would see when I turned around. There was an absolutely gorgeous 11-year-old girl with wavy, fiery reddish hair, huge blue eyes, and a presence that actually glowed. She appeared, at least in body, to be severely disabled. But I knew better!

Lorrin was in a wheelchair, barely able to lift her hands or legs. Her head lolled to one side, and at first glance it appeared as if she was completely unaware of her surroundings. As I approached her I looked into her eyes, and I could see that Lorrin was in fact quite present, very aware, and trapped only by her physicality. With permission, I touched her gently. To me, her energy field was like floating in liquid love. I asked her if she was one of the little girls who had been talking with me for a while. Her eyebrows went up ("Yes!"). I thought so. Lorrin and I chatted for a while telepathically. As she and I talked, her mom, Karen, and I laughed about the situation as her daughter and I did our thing. Mom was great. Talking with Lorrin and her mom was pure bliss. We interacted for 15 or 20 minutes until there was a rush of people who filled the aisles on their way to the next scheduled lectures. Lorrin and her mom went to hear a lecture as well.

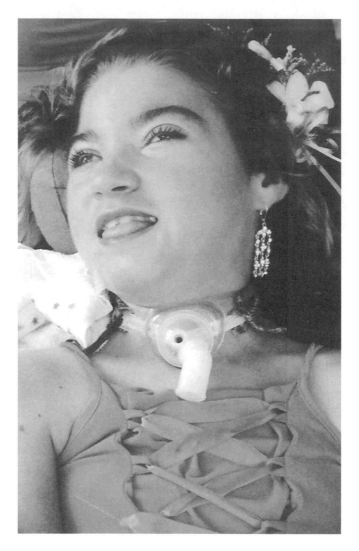

Figure 9. Lorrin.

That night as I was sleeping, my dreams were interrupted and I was suddenly awakened. As I sat up, my head filled with images of Lorrin. At first I thought I was dreaming, but as I realized I was upright and completely awake, I knew that Lorrin was communicating with me. The amazing thing about traveling out of body is that there is no time or space, so what did it matter to Lorrin that it was the middle of the night? Lorrin's favorite singer is LeAnn Rimes, and her greatest desire is to dance joyfully, like a ballerina, free of her restrictive body. Now wide awake, I literally watched her performance in my mind's eye. Lorrin filled my mind with images of her dancing. She wore ballet slippers and was up on her toes, lifting and moving her arms gracefully as if they were weightless wings, and spanning the air around her as she twirled and leapt across the dance floor. In the visions Lorrin sent to me there were mirrors everywhere, and as I looked in every direction I saw infinite reflections of her beautiful self flying across the floor unencumbered. I laughed aloud and loved every minute of her sweet recital. Here was another splendid creature with a sense of humor! When Lorrin and her mom came around the next day, I teased Lorrin about visiting me in the night. She raised her eyebrows ("Yes!") and smiled. All through the rest of the weekend as I went about my days, I was often interrupted with telepathic messages that I should "go here" or "go there." Every single time I spontaneously acted on those commands, I ran into—guess who? Lorrin! It actually got to be a joke between my little friend's mom and me. We had a great time together.

In a later conversation with Karen, Lorrin's mom, we spoke of Lorrin's giftedness and how people gravitate to her. She radiates complete love from within, and she is gorgeous in all of her dysfunction. Karen said that the hardest part about being a parent of such a uniquely gifted child is getting past the idea of seeing her child as broken and in need of fixing. After all, it is just the outside appearance, the physical functioning, that is affected. The inside is just fine, if only people could hear.

Karen later described some of the extraordinary effects that Lorrin has on those who meet her. For instance, three different people have spontaneously quit smoking immediately and successfully after being with Lorrin. None of them intended to quit prior to meeting her. Lorrin seems to have inherent abilities to communicate and instigate certain kinds of healing to some people.

Children like Lorrin are a great lesson to us all. Often when we encounter people and circumstances that don't fit into our construct of "normal," we reflexively move into revulsion or fear because we have been socialized to feel that what is different is frightening. We do not necessarily always have the skills we need to be of comfort and grace in those situations. The gifts that reside within our special children are beyond measure. Let's not miss the boat!

BRIAN

(Note from the author: This story will no doubt challenge the reader's sense of reality even further because it is very unusual. It is because of its extreme difference that I have included it here. The Children of Now will always continue to challenge our sense of reality!)

The uniqueness of the Children of Now spans across time and space and into realities with which most of us are not familiar. This ability to cross time and space unhindered is very real, and it is fascinating to experience. It requires letting go of all of what we thought we knew about perception and reality—and there is nothing wrong with that. We have a lot to learn from our Beautiful Silent Ones.

A few weeks after meeting Lorrin and Karen in Arizona, I went to Minnesota for a private gathering of powerful light workers. The entire trip was magical from the beginning. Our hostess, Nancy, e-mailed me and asked if I would participate in a private ceremony at the headwaters of the Mississippi River, at Lake Itaska. The timing was perfect, as it was immediately after Hurricane Katrina had devastated the Gulf Coast. Nancy arranged flights for my husband and me, and off we went. I did not know Nancy prior to her e-mail, and just assumed she knew me from my newsletter list like most others who e-mail me. Pure inner guidance took me there.

The morning after our arrival, I overheard someone asking Nancy how she had managed to gather such a stellar group of people, and Nancy basically said that it was her job to call the "family" together. She explained that her concept about the weekend gathering was about healing and regeneration, so that all of us could go back out into the world refreshed and rested enough to share our gifts. As others began to gather for breakfast, I approached Nancy and asked her if she was on my newsletter list. She wasn't. Now I was really curious. Her intuition had told her to contact me, so she did. Although I felt that something else was coming, I wasn't sure where this was all going, and so I left it at that.

For years I have written and spoken in what I call the language of light. It is a conceptual language that is very powerful for healing and teaching because it is pure energy. The light language is comprised of living symbols that contain entire teachings on many levels. At times I have even found myself thinking in this language. I have often felt somewhat alone in this ability; however, over the years I have found others who are fluent in the same language. Recently I have met others who have begun to receive this gift as well.

That morning at the breakfast table, I made acquaintance with Chief Golden Eagle (a.k.a. Standing Elk) of the Lakota Sioux Nation, and his beautiful wife, Maria. Golden Eagle and I immediately bonded as we launched into a conversation that ultimately (and perfectly) led to the symbols. As we talked, it was obvious that the chief was quite familiar with the symbols. I asked him excitedly, "You understand the symbols too?"

Without a word, he got up out of his chair and went out to his truck, and when he came back he handed me an entire notebook filled with the very same symbols that I had been working with for years. I turned on my computer and began to show the chief a set of cards I had been designing with, of course, the symbols. We were extremely excited to find each other! We talked a lot about our translations, and about the differences in positioning or direction that change the meaning of the symbols. (Reference to the living symbols can be found in the Nag Hammadi codices in the Gospel of Truth. These ancient documents, discovered in the 1940s, were found in clay vessels hidden in a cave in Nag Hammadi at the edge of the Red Sea. They are apparently part of the Gnostic Library that was considered heretical at the time they were hidden more than 2,000 years ago.)

The next day, Bennie LeBeau (a.k.a. Blue Thunder), another beautiful and warm-hearted spiritual being, showed up with more pieces of the puzzle. (Bennie is of the Shoshone Nation, and spends most of his time performing ceremonies based upon grid formations and sacred sites to heal the Earth. As he reconnects the sacred grids, Bennie heals the water as well; springs that dried up long ago have sprung to life, and the flow of water continues long after Bennie has gone. Where there were droughts, rain and moisture are abundant again.) Bennie and I began to converse, and pretty soon the subject came around to the symbols. It was no surprise that Bennie knew them too. At some point during our conversation the chief joined in, and Nancy stood in the background with a well-deserved, self-satisfied smirk on her face. It was quickly becoming clear why some of us had gathered there.

I began to tell Bennie and the chief about William, and how he communicates with me telepathically, and about some of the other children who have contacted me as well. William had told me that he also knows the symbols, so I outlined my experiences with him to Golden Eagle and Bennie. Nancy overheard what I said about William not physically speaking, and she rushed over and grabbed my arm. She was talking so fast I had a hard time making sense of her words. "You have to come and see this. I thought it was a really smart baby that did this but now I get it. Look! I bought this at a craft show—it was the child's grandfather who had the booth!" Nancy was very excited. "The grandfather said the child didn't talk yet and that all he does is write these symbols. Grandpa wouldn't say much else; it seemed that talking about his grandson was uncomfortable for him. I assumed that the child was really small, and now I realize that maybe I misunderstood what the grandfather meant."

With that, Nancy reached up to the side of her kitchen cabinet and pulled out a most amazing piece of pottery. It was shaped like a saucer, and had symbols in concentric rings all around the edges—with a different set inside of the first set, and another inside of that—and a middle section that depicted a spiral design. As soon as I saw the saucer, the orb consciousnesses of the children in my field started chattering at me all at once. They were very excited.

They told me this boy had been lost and that we could help him. Boy, life just keeps getting stranger and more exciting!

Of course, the next thing to do was to get in touch with the maker of the saucer and talk with him. Because the saucer was randomly purchased at a craft fair, we had no idea how to contact the family, so we had to do this telepathically. Even though the children were great at contacting me, I was still new at all of this. I wasn't sure how it would go, but, as usual, what happened was amazing. We set a space in which everyone could gather. As I held the saucer, I opened my awareness, and suddenly information began to pour into my head. The maker of the saucer came into my field in orb form and began to talk with me. We will call him Brian. I listened carefully to what Brian said and shared his words with everyone in the group.

We asked Brian why he made this particular piece. He said that he had made it because he knew that one day the right person would see it, recognize the message, and contact him—and it had finally happened! (This was another one of those moments in life when you just know that everything you thought you knew just took a major shift. Reality expands, and there are no seat belts, so there is no point in trying to hold on for the ride. The momentum will keep you where you need to be!) As I turned the saucer around in my hands, I began to notice certain patterns within the design. There were many levels of different types of symbols, beginning from the outside edge and moving to the center.

As I rotated the saucer in my hands, Brian's parallel aspect began to talk to me telepathically. The story he had to tell me was mind-boggling. He said, "You have to read this holographically. Look at the numbers first." So I began to count the marks and the symbols. Brian explained about the genetics of "his people." He told me that part of the code that he built into his pottery creation explains their DNA structure. He said that the people of his planet actually have four strands of DNA (compared to our two), and exactly double the number of genetic codons that human beings have. (A codon is a specific sequence of three adjacent bases on a strand of DNA or RNA that provides the genetic code information for a particular amino acid. Basically, they tell our DNA how to work and communicate back to the RNA. Codons tell our bodies when to stop and start the myriad of processes that constantly occur within us. Certain sets of codons contribute to anomalous activities in our bodies as well.)

Figure 10. A frontal view of the pottery saucer.
It is difficult to see in the photograph, but it is curved
like a very shallow dish (caption courtesy of Nancy Kuhta).

Figure 11. The pottery saucer in greater detail.

Brian told us that his parallel aspect was from the planet Steara. He explained that the DNA of the Stearans has holographic aspects that communicate much like liquid crystals. Liquid crystals create a fluid field of energy in which communication is immediate and pure, and able to contain huge amounts of information in tiny formats. He said that our DNA is just as capable as theirs, just not as evolved. He went on to share that the DNA of the Stearans is capable of intentional and complete harmonized communications in parallel realities. He said that this genetic structure also gives them the ability to dematerialize their bodies for intergalactic travel. In other words, they have the ability to break down their bodies into their most essential and basic formats, and ride the channels through time and space to other realities, planets, star systems, galaxies, and so on. Brian also told me that his people were highly advanced technologically, and that they had learned to travel in the "in betweens." This is in the same vein as wormholes, but the "in betweens" are even more intricate pathways that require travelers to dematerialize to a particulate level. This is amazing—intentional and self-instigated "beam me up, Scotty"!

As Brian "talked," he showed me visually what he described for everyone—my head became filled with images of another planet, the "in betweens," and particulate reduction and assimilation. He showed me how the Stearans can excite their particles with their consciousness, causing the particles to separate into different harmonic relationships, and how this enables them to ride the "in betweens" as energy fields to intentional destinations in time and space. It was as if I had jumped right into the special effects of a science fiction film, with Brian as the director.

Brian said that the Stearans are far more evolved than human beings. They don't use words to communicate because they don't need to; they communicate telepathically or with symbols. These symbols carry full sets of information and are not to be read individually. Brian said that the symbols are sets of harmonic frequencies, similar to our energy fields. The symbols on the saucer tell a fantastic story of planetary struggles, Brian's galactic lineage, and even star coordinates.

Indeed, Brian told of a solar system in the central part of our galaxy where a catastrophic event took place. Apparently, the solar system, Andion, revolves in elliptical orbit around three suns. (The rotation around the suns was a long process, and the days on his planet were not like ours here on Earth.) The orbit of Steara was forever changed by a black hole in the center of the galaxy. (A black hole is actually a balance mechanism between universes. As our universe expands, the black hole drains off excess energy into a parallel universe. Black holes are present in all universes, and this system of "checks and

balances" maintains equilibrium among levels of reality.)
Due to the imbalance created by the heavy gravitational
pull of the black hole, Brian's home planet was pulled out
of its normal orbit. The tilt of the axis of the planet created
a pole shift, which in turn initiated a wobble effect.
Magnetic and true north changed, and the gravitational
properties of the planet changed as well. Instead of an
elliptical path around the three suns, the planet's orbit
became an out-of-balance looping pattern. It was similar
to a rocket without a gyroscope to balance its trajectory.
Steara collided with a maverick celestial body. Destruction
of Steara was immediate and complete.

There were 13 planets in the Andion solar system. Now
there are 12.

At the time of the planetary destruction there were
large numbers of Stearans out "on assignment." Because
they were not on Steara at the time of the disaster, they
survived, but with the dilemma of no home to return to.
Brian went on to tell us that there is a planet in their solar
system that has a green atmosphere that is not habitable
for the Stearans but would be habitable to others. He said
that the air is not compatible to their bodies, which have
substantial amounts of the minerals iridium and
molybdenum. The prevalence of these two minerals assists
the Stearans to work in harmony with the universe.
Humans, on the other hand, are carbon based. Brian also
said that the Stearans may seem like anomalies to us, but it
is humans who are the anomalies, because we are way
behind most other civilizations in our evolution. He went
on to say that the Stearans' brains are fully wired, and that
they are capable of unimaginable technology.

The culture on Steara was structured for the good of
the whole. In other words, everyone acted in the best
interest of the planet and each other. Brian said that we
on Earth are on a "bad path" because we don't pay
attention to the things that are important to our survival.

He said that the people of Earth constantly fight about nothing:

> People on Earth in large part are like spoiled children. Everyone thinks everyone else is responsible for their happiness or to blame for their misery. This kind of thinking is separation from the good of the whole, and it won't work indefinitely. No one is better than anyone else, and if you don't change that way of thinking, you will burn yourselves out. Most human beings have such an exalted view of themselves in relation to all others that they have closed the door to their conscious access to greater reality. This can be changed. We learned from our mistakes, and if you are willing to listen we can help you. There are much cleaner and easier alternatives to the kinds of fuel you currently use. What you use now pollutes every aspect of your environment and creates an imbalance on the Earth. And the supply is limited.

There was more from Brian, but the important issue here is that, somewhere out there, there is a child with extreme capabilities and fantastic technology to offer the world. I asked Brian to find a way to come forward like the other kids have, particularly to Nancy or those who live in his area, so that he can receive more support for who he is. Much to my delight, Brian eventually appeared in person with his grandmother!

Our Beautiful Silent Ones are deceiving to our senses. While they appear to be extremely limited on the outside, they have worlds to offer us if only we will open ourselves to hear them. The first step is to be open to the possibilities of alternate realities, because they do exist. The next step is to let go of perceptions of control and just allow ourselves to be in the moment. When we do, we are more likely to pick up on infinite numbers of other things that we have been missing all of our lives. Leave it to the children to teach us the complexities of creation from the innocence of their being!

THE TRANSITIONAL CHLDREN

CHAPTER 10

The Transitional Children are a very special group of beings who came to Earth after the Indigo Children, and are roughly between the ages of 16 and 22 at this writing. Caught in the crossfire of evolving forces, the Transitional Children came to Earth with a mixed bag of energies. It is as if, at the time of their becoming, a little of every type of energy was dumped into their natures and stirred up. They aren't Indigos, but they do carry some of the Indigo energy (for example, they have a great sense that the paradigms in which they live are not of truth). They aren't Crystalline, but parts of their fields work in the same way as those of the Crystalline Children. In many ways, the Transitionals are often just as sensitive and gifted. They aren't Star Children, yet they carry many of those attributes as well. Some of them are brilliant, inherently knowing many things about the Earth and beyond.

The Transitional Children sometimes act as "bridges" between the energy forces, and at times this can be a fascinating phenomenon. For instance, a child who is fairly balanced, and who carries both the Indigo and Crystalline patterns of energy, may appear to be rebellious, but in a deliciously creative way. Case in point: A young man from Norfolk, Virginia, named Chris Garnett joined PETA, an animal rights activist group for the prevention of cruelty to animals. The group had been running a campaign against the Kentucky Fried Chicken fast-food chain of restaurants with allegations of cruelty to chickens. Chris became so impassioned with the cause that he recently made national news when he legally changed his name to Kentucky-Fried-Cruelty-dot-com. In this case, we see that Chris has the paradigm-busting sense of the Indigo combined with the socially conscious Crystalline energy. He said that his new name "never fails to spark a discussion."

Another amazing example of the combined Indigo and Crystalline energy forces is 16-year-old Farris Hassan. Farris gained international attention with a solo odyssey to Iraq. Farris's family is from Iraq, and has lived in the United States for 30 years. Scheduled for a school field trip over the Christmas holiday, Farris packed his bags and left as planned. Instead of joining his classmates, however, Farris took his passport and $1,800 and detoured on his own all the way to Iraq. Once there, he e-mailed his parents of his whereabouts. Farris has been studying immersion journalism in high school, and his intention was to plunge himself into the lives of the Iraqi people for a clearer understanding of the war and its effects on them. Farris also wanted to witness the history-making parliamentary elections in December of 2005. Even though the State

Department was warning Americans not to visit Iraq, Farris entered the war zone in Baghdad with no problem. Upon arrival, he presented himself to some AP reporters who were staying in a hotel. "I thought I'd go the extra mile for that, or rather, a few thousand miles," he told them. The reporters ultimately gained assistance from the U.S. military, and troops escorted Farris back home. He was met by a throng of reporters upon his arrival. Another case of Indigo and Crystalline energies combining to yield social awareness and amazing achievements!

No two sets of Transitional energies are the same. The children who are affected by the new energies react in a multitude of ways, and this does not always yield as humorous or positive an outcome as it did for the young men described here. Some of these children will seem hyperactive or unstable due to the confusion within their overall energy systems. Basically, the same energy fluctuations in their fields that bring exceptional giftedness can cause a myriad of problems. This situation also causes extreme variations in emotional stability and coping ability.

Transitional Children have amazing perception on many or even all levels of reality, yet they often lack the skills or ability to logically integrate those experiences into their everyday lives. Because of this, many of them become angry, frustrated, or even sick. They have a cosmic sense that all is not right in their world, but, because of the barrage of intuitive and otherworldly input they constantly receive, they cannot seem to ferret out the answers or solutions to their feelings and perceptions. What they see and experience outside of third-dimensional reality is often so bizarre that these kids shut down communications with their families and friends and begin to internalize their experiences.

Some of the Transitional Children see reality in much different ways than most people. Etheric guides, angels, spirits of those who have passed on, and even what they sometimes describe as demons (which are actually nothing more than lower-dimensional beings) are seen and experienced by these children constantly. Indeed, some of the Transitional Children I have worked with have expressed frustration that they never have any privacy, because there is always a crowd of otherworldly beings with them. As they are growing up, the Transitional Children often do not feel safe. They are frequently plagued with a sense of the presence of these dark beings, and they feel that the beings are there to influence them or even hurt them. And many of the children tell no one. Day after day they live in fear and confusion. The more disturbing the situation becomes, the greater the sense of gloom and doom. Some of these kids actually begin to believe that they are influenced or possessed by dark entities. In most cases, that is not true.

The Transitional Children do not understand that their visions are simply manifestations of other planes of reality. Because no one else can see these things, the child starts to believe that he or she is not normal, and a profound sense of aloneness creeps in. Thus, they become victims of their giftedness. Everything feels weighty and earth-shattering to the Transitional Kids, and as they enter their teens, many of them develop the belief that there is something really wrong with them. The perception that they are somehow flawed is devastating to these kids. Their moods become dark, and they begin to demonstrate these feelings through their artwork, in how they decorate their rooms, with their clothing, and even in their activities. Self-destructive behavior is common. If they lean toward the dark energies, they may become involved in using illegal drugs and/or alcohol. Some appear to be depressed or even suicidal. After a while they may even become sociopaths, because they have become numb and stopped caring. To these kids, the illusion of darkness outweighs the light.

Most of us have filters that keep us from seeing and feeling everything all of the time, but these children do not. Let's face it—"normal" children have a hard enough time coping with the fluctuations in their bodies and minds during adolescence. Factor in an entirely different set of feelings and perceptions, such as the ones the Transitional Children have, and a new and more problematic dimension is added. Not all of the Transitional Children are inundated with these kinds of feelings and experiences, but those who are, are often affected to the extreme. Some doctors would label this as psychotic behavior, but it is not.

Some of the Transitional Children project a façade of omnipotence, of being greater than everyone and everything else. They project this persona when they relate to others, and eventually they stop respecting authority. Even the Transitional Children who choose a more positive route often become overwhelmed and sick—losing weight, exhibiting signs of depression, and displaying physical symptoms that cannot be explained medically. It is as if they grieve for the entire world. They are overcome by their gifts and lost in their journeys.

As with the Crystallines, many of the Transitional Children demonstrate extreme sensitivity—they feel and notice everything. The mixed energy fields of these children contribute to the amplification of normal sensitivity. Imagine that everything you feel is multiplied to the power of 10, all of the time, every day of your life, good or bad. Hyperaware, hypersensitive, "hyper" everything—that is how these kids feel. Emotional hurts are magnified way beyond what "normal" people feel. Many of the Transitional Children are very artistic, and they use their art to express the depth and breadth of their feelings in dramatic ways.

One young woman I worked with several years ago expressed her frustration about never having any privacy. No matter where she was or what she was doing, she would always see demonic beings, angels, and guides. When she went for walks, she said it was as if she had a multidimensional entourage. She told me that, in a way, she actually felt as if she was being stalked, and it frightened her. In her giftedness, she was never alone. Because of her experiences, the young woman began to know things that she didn't share even with her mom, with whom she was quite close. (Mom was quite supportive of her daughter, and was the impetus to our working together.) The young woman didn't feel as if she could share her episodes with anyone because they were so bizarre that she regularly questioned her sanity. She had become frightened and unsure.

This young woman gradually became quite sick, and no one could figure out why. When I first met her, she had been ill for months. She was thin with very dark patches under her eyes, and her vitality was very low. None of her medical tests brought answers. She was sick and tired—literally! All that it took for this beautiful one to turn her life around was for someone to tell her that what she was experiencing was real, plain and simple. We talked for hours, and as she expressed her experiences to me, I told her, "If you are experiencing these things, then you must *also* know about...." And she looked at me with wide eyes and said that she hadn't told anyone about those things, so how could I know? She was amazed and relieved to know that others are similarly gifted. After our session my young friend became much more social, began to physically heal, and started to enjoy her life without the burden of the hidden fear that she had carried for so long. She even found a boyfriend.

The Transitional Children who hide their feelings and experiences get tired. There are physical reasons for this. Their heightened sensitivity depletes basic minerals within their systems that are vital to life. Magnesium depletes first, then calcium. Other minerals, such as aluminum, begin to plug into cell receptors, even though they don't belong there. After a while, the body becomes toxic or underfunctioning. Being in the presence of some of these kids for the first time feels a bit like being sucked down a drain together, because they have become so very tired. One who is sensitive to energy can actually feel the constant drain from these kids. To pull them up and to balance them takes special patience on the part of the healing practitioner. The Transitional Children are also prone to infections and other illnesses that mysteriously begin and end, often without definitive diagnosis from the medical community. I call this "cosmic illness," because it comes from a source that is beyond third-dimensional biological sources. Transitional Kids in particular need self-validation. They need to know that there are others like them, and that they aren't alone in their experiences. That awareness alone can mean the difference between a child stepping back into life positively, and literally not surviving.

It seems as though these kids tend to polarize one way or another—they either become empowered, or they *perceive* power because of their giftedness. Put another way, they either grow in their giftedness, or they begin to think that their giftedness can be used to gain power over others in malevolent ways. Which way the children go is a choice, but it is one made of experience. More often than not, I find that the choice made is directly related to what kind of support system the children have. There are those who, when supported and nurtured, step into their giftedness and grow with it. The kids who hide their sensitivity and awareness, on the other hand, become disturbed or sick over time. They feel helpless and hopeless, and some of them step into power gleaned from negative influences. Many of them become self-abusive or violent toward others.

BRITTANY

The first Transitional Child with whom I worked was a 15-year-old girl who was referred to me by a psychologist friend of mine. I will call her Brittany. Because of family issues, Brittany had turned her amazing gifts toward pure meanness and the practice of witchcraft. She was playing seriously with black magic. She was a powerful being whose energy force filled the room in an uncomfortable way as it sought to overcome everyone around her. Brittany's mother was obviously cowed by her daughter, and she sat silent and still as her daughter spoke loudly and with profanity. Mom didn't dare contradict her daughter or even give an appearance of opposition. I found out later that the young woman often acted out, directing her anger and violence toward her family. At that time, everyone was afraid of her.

Brittany had actually started her own witch's coven, which practiced dark magic—mostly during the night. She and her group were sexually promiscuous and shared deviant behaviors. There was no discernment about when, where, or with whom these acts took place. She seemed to see nothing wrong in her behavior—in fact, she seemed quite proud of her actions. Brittany and her coven of friends roamed the roads at night, doing pretty terrible things by most people's standards. She thought nothing of hurting people, because she had decided by then that violence and threatening behavior amplified her power. She had found that she and some of her friends had the power to influence the thoughts and actions of others, and she used her gift as a weapon to manipulate people. Brittany realized that her telepathy could be used to her gain, and she used it fluently and regularly. As she learned to harness her giftedness in this way, she became more and more deceived about her own greatness. Her family was terrified of her. No one stopped her from going out or restricted her activities in any way. Parenting skills lacked considerably. Generally speaking, the family as a unit was seriously dysfunctional on many levels. One could argue that Brittany was born into this family in order for growth and learning to occur on both sides.

When her mom brought her in for an appointment, Brittany recoiled from me. Her vocabulary was filled with profanity, and she created huge energetic blocks like a fortress around her. She felt like pure meanness, and she breathed the stuff born of deep anger. Feeling frustration about the fact that neither the daughter nor the mother would communicate with me beyond pleasantries, I decided to talk to Brittany on her own terms. I mirrored to her what she was showing to me, meanness and all. Surprised at my display of tough love, she responded positively and ultimately agreed to my working with her. Brittany's energy field was a conglomeration of many types of energy and had little organization to it. Changes were made, and the session completed. She actually responded very well by the end of the session. The child who had come in so meanly roaring like a lion left that day with a serene smile and a huge hug for me.

Unfortunately, as time went on, Brittany chose the lower roads once again. She attempted suicide and was hospitalized. She began to channel very negative entities. There was little help for this kind of situation, because she had been allowed to continue the game for too long. I later received a call that her sister, who was only a year or two younger, was in jeopardy as well, exhibiting similar behaviors. Another extremely gifted child without a net to catch her when she falls. Brittany ultimately became tired of life and everything that came with it. She became very sick and passed away, bless her heart and soul. She had so much to offer, but could never seem to find her niche in a world that did not understand her. This was clearly a case in which the family, faced with a powerful child, did not possess the skills to nurture or support the child in constructive ways based upon her giftedness. Instead they became overwhelmed. All of the professional help in the world will not change a situation unless *everyone* involved chooses to participate.

Sometimes none of what society has to offer fits the desperate needs of a child like Brittany. Ultimately, some of these children just give up. It is a sad commentary on society that we cannot seem to embrace those with such vast differences; instead, we label these children dysfunctional, until they feel as if that dysfunction is their identity. In this writer's opinion, the greatest reason for this failing is a fear of what is "abnormal." What if Brittany had been supported in her giftedness from the beginning? What if she had learned to feel fantastic about herself? What if? Now we will never know.

HEATHER

Another Transitional Child came to me at the request of her mother, who is a friend and colleague of mine, and she turned out quite differently. When Heather and her mom came for the appointment, I could see that the girl didn't really want to be there—partly, I think, because she had known me for several years and was perhaps a bit embarrassed. I hugged them both as they arrived and proceeded to take them into a private area.

Heather was 16 and had gotten involved in drugs and promiscuous behavior, and was also exhibiting violent conduct. She thought nothing of the fact that she had cut someone with a knife. In fact, she laughed when she told me about it. Because she was so aware of other realities, and because she had gotten into negative behavior patterns, Heather had decided that she was possessed by some sort of demon. She said that she had a lot of thoughts that seemed to come from somewhere else. She often felt mean and concluded that her malice was instigated by dark entities. She said that she couldn't be held responsible for being possessed. Basically, she was telling me that nothing she did was her fault, but rather the fault of those who were talking in her head all of the time. She wasn't willing to own the fact that she was making bad choices in her life.

I sat quietly and listened, watching her change from the girl I knew to someone who personified absolute meanness. As I listened, I realized that Heather had convinced herself of these things because she didn't have any answers. No one had answers for what she was experiencing. Further, Heather's dad had left the family several years prior. That event seemed to confirm to Heather that she must not be wanted or loved anyway. Armed with this conviction, she was proving her lack of worth from within her giftedness. In this case, her hypersensitivity (characteristic of the Transitional Child) had blown her feelings way out of proportion, and she was acting negatively on them.

After listening to Heather for a while, I began to engage her. As I did, I often switched tactics in order to keep her a bit off balance. She was trying to portray a persona that didn't fit, and I wasn't buying it. As she began to talk more about being possessed, I stopped her and mirrored to her exactly the same negativity that she sent my way.

"Bullshit," I said. "If you really were possessed, you wouldn't have been able to hug me on your way in here! You are just making excuses to justify your behavior and I am not buying it for one minute." Briefly her eyes widened, and then the meanness came back. It was quite impressive to be on the receiving end of her hateful looks. Heather continued to try very hard to convince me that there was an entity making her do things that were bad. Next, with the complete opposite energy of pure love, I told her that I knew who she really was, and that the Heather I knew wouldn't possibly accept that kind of powerlessness. Back and forth we went until finally she agreed to do some energy work with me.

When we began her session, I noticed that there were in fact dark entities hanging around ethereally, but they had been drawn in during Heather's drug use and the other behaviors that had validated her self-loathing. The entities had not caused her poor choices, but were a result of them. As is typical with the Transitional Children, Heather's energy field was all askew and chaotic, with errant pathways throughout the energy system. Her energies were also very diverse—not Indigo, not Crystalline, nothing in particular and everything at once.

As we worked I spoke to her of love and of unconditional acceptance. I shared with her that she was none of the negative things she had come to believe. I told her that I saw her as beautiful. I really meant that. I saw and felt Heather's pain, and mirrored it to her through compassion and with love. I talked with her about her gifts, and expressed gentle understanding of knowing what it is like to be different. I also talked to Heather about love, and what a difference the force of love can make in vanquishing anger and self-loathing. I told Heather that I was not willing to accept any assertion from her that she was anything less than perfection. I told her that I knew that she was a beautiful person. We talked about many of her otherworldly experiences, and I was able explain each, giving her clarification about what was happening. It was a great relief to her. Heather was beginning to see that having awareness didn't necessarily mean ownership. One of the more difficult problems that challenge these kids is that they often feel responsible for their insights, their experiences, their visions, their precognitions, and so on. They become victims of their gifts—at least in their thinking. They are not responsible for the information that comes to them. Usually, once they find someone who will be truthful with them and can understand the reality of their experiences, these children will do a complete about-face because their fears and concerns have been assuaged.

During some of the more intense work that we did together, Heather sometimes seemed to wander off in her mind as she digested our conversation. She was listening, but her ability to take in the truth was hampered in the face of her negativity. Ultimately, however, she accepted change. Her energy field was balanced, and the blockages within it were removed. From that day forward she turned her life around completely—she has been clean and sober, and has learned to see herself from a positive perspective. Her life has begun to reflect those positive changes back to her. Because she is living in a positive fashion, positive changes have occurred. She is well loved by everyone who knows her, she is using her high intelligence to create plans for her future, and she is choosing great environments in which to work and play. Heather has become a nanny for several families, and she relishes the fact that the children she works with really love her, as do their families. Heather continues to be supported by her own family as well. She is 21 years old now and determined to live a comfortable life without all of the negative behaviors. She has stuck with her plan very well, and, personally, I am very proud of her!

The Transitional Children have a tendency to become so angry that they have difficulty thinking rationally. The method I have found that works best with them involves a bit of "shapeshifting" in tone and posturing. Sometimes the only way to get their attention is to give back to them what they are giving—in other words, meet them on their own terms and be a mirror to them. The trick is not to be like them, only to mirror their behavior. One can do this firmly without falling into the ugly side of that behavior. Once their attention is gained (usually due to the shock of having a professional act that way!), loving truth can be communicated. Their heightened perception recognizes the truth and responds to it.

Children learn from adults and their contemporaries, as well as from today's media, about deception and self-destructive behaviors, and they often use what they learn to validate feelings that their gifts make them nobodies or freaks. These children must be validated and encouraged, and shown how to harness their gifts toward positive growth. Most of all, their communication skills must be honed and utilized. When a child begins to shut out others, it is often because his or her coping skills are lacking, and it feels safer to contain strong feelings than it does to risk exposure and vulnerability. It may also mean that he or she not being heard. A child who doesn't feel heard by others is a child who begins to believe that he or she is not worth hearing. These kids must be validated even when we can't seem to understand their experiences. Our lack of understanding doesn't mean that they are any less real! There is nothing to fear; heightened awareness is not contagious.

Moderate structure is also helpful to the Transitional Children—not a restrictive set of demands, but a loosely organized set of activities and goals in which they participate. When a child knows what to expect, there is comfort in that. Most of the Transitional Kids who are having difficulty live in homes where everyone is too busy to notice each other, or broken or dysfunctional homes that lack communication and healthy life skills. When there is a format in which to live, that format tells the children that someone really does care. It gives the children small ways to measure their safety in a predictable environment, and self-validation when they accomplish something within the set guidelines.

The Transitional Children are not just rebellious teens. Deep down they are scared—of what they see, what they hear, and what they know, all of which no one else seems to understand. Listen to them. Don't judge them because they seem to have strange ideas and perceptions. Encourage open, honest conversation. We have a lot to learn from them!

ANGELS *on* EARTH

CHAPTER 11

Throughout history, we have read or heard about angels who come to Earth to be of assistance to us. This surprisingly common phenomenon was aptly and vividly illustrated when I narrowly avoided having a car accident some time ago. I was driving down a road at a fast speed, when all of a sudden I realized that there was a large piece of wood in front of me. It was a long square post of some kind. Before I realized what was happening, I ran over the wood, and as I did, both of the tires on the driver's side of my car blew out. From that point on, everything seemed to be in slow motion. One millisecond at a time, I was aware of every intricate part of the progression of events.

"Angels!" I pleaded, "Help me!" The driver's side of my car was off the ground, and I was careening forward at an excessive speed on two wheels. I was also in the fast lane and needed to move over to the shoulder of the road without wrecking my car, hitting someone else, or completely losing control of the car. The balance of the vehicle felt dangerously precarious. Faster than I could comprehend, I began to receive instructions that calmly spoke to me. "Easy," the voice said. "Don't panic. Turn your steering wheel ever so slightly this way, not too much or the car will flip." I could see that! "Now, use the momentum of your car to steer it. Ease over to the other lane—now! That's it. Now touch the brakes gently so that the car stops in a straight line—good, good. Now, pull off of the road and come to a stop."

In spite of my predicament, I felt calm and perfectly guided as I followed the instructions. As I got out of the car and saw the extent of the damage, I began to shake all over. The adrenaline that was pumping through my system was maximized. Automatically, I went to the trunk for my spare tire and jack, only to realize a second or two later that I had only one spare. I was too wobbly from the shock of the accident to even try to use the jack anyway.

"I need an angel, God," I said, as I held onto the car for support. As I finished my prayer, I looked up to see a van turning around in the median and heading my way. The van pulled up and a kindly older gentleman got out. Even in my distress, I couldn't help but notice a glow around my rescuer. He was very quiet, but the few words he did say were calming. He spoke only enough to communicate what was necessary and nothing more. He helped me with everything, and before he left, I asked his name. He gave me one, and said that he lived in a certain community that I was familiar with. Later, when I tried to find him to thank him for assisting me, I found that he didn't exist.

The address didn't exist. No one had heard of my gentle hero. He wasn't of this Earth—my prayers had been answered, and an angel had come.

There are countless stories such as this in which angels come to the rescue and then disappear just as quickly, never to be heard from again. This type of angelic interaction is typical of guardian angels.

However, the angels I will describe here are very different. They are being born in human form, wings and all. Their wings aren't visible to everyone, but there are some who can see them. There is an etheric quality to these children, which words are insufficient to describe. The few I have met are having a very hard time. They are cosmically sad for humanity. They do not feel as if they truly belong in our world and at the same time, they know of God, Spirit, and the Light, and they experience the depth of feeling that comes from that knowing to their very core.

MICHAEL

About seven or eight years ago I received a call from a good friend, who asked me to talk with a young man she knew. He was in his early 20s. She felt he might be in trouble, and she told me that I would understand when I spoke with him. At the time I was still working on sorting out my own awakening, and I was very excited to hear the story this young man had to tell. I will call him Michael.

Before I could call him, he called me. Michael was a bit timid with me at first. He was on the other side of the country and alone. I could feel sadness oozing through the telephone. As he and I talked, Michael began to open more and more to me and tell me his story, and, as he did, I wanted to reach through the phone and hold him.

I have wings. I feel like I have to go out into the
world and share messages of love. I have literally
been wandering around the world for the last
year. I went to Europe and walked barefoot
everywhere I went. I can't stand wearing shoes
because it is like having my feet in a box. I need
for my feet to feel the ground because it helps
me stay anchored in earthly reality. I usually feel
as if I am barely here. I really need help. I had
some wonderful experiences in my travels,
especially when I went to Padre Pio's. (Padre
Pio was a devout priest who was known for
healing others miraculously. He had the stigmata,
the marks of Christ's crucifixion, on his body.)
When I was there, I could feel the light, the
love, his miracles—and I was comfortable. I
managed to gain possession of one of his gloves.
The energy contained in his glove is a treasure
and a good reminder to me that one person can
affect many others. I don't know what to do or
where to go next. I know that I must share what
I know. I know that I will touch people—heal
people in their bodies, hearts, and souls—but
right now I am lost and alone. Can you give me
any information that would help?

I closed my eyes and looked at this being energetically.
He truly did have wings! They were white with a golden
glow that undulated around the edges. His entire energy
field was so nearly perfect that to gaze upon him, even
ethereally, was very difficult because his brightness was so
great. God, another reality shift! I had had some experience
by then of wings and angels, but I hadn't really expected
to hear from one on the phone. We talked for several
hours, and as we did, his profound sadness permeated his
words. He was so ungrounded that even participating in
logical conversation was difficult for him. His spirit was so
pure. To Michael, the injury that humanity had inflicted

upon itself was so great that he felt too small and powerless to make any positive changes here on Earth.

With human insight, I helped him to better understand compassion, love, and choices. I spoke with him about personal safety, and how his vulnerability was both a treasure and a difficulty. He was so innocent, so pure, that he couldn't understand why everyone couldn't understand God, the light, and love. For a while I spoke with him only of mundane things, such his body's need for food and sleep. He was having a hard time sustaining his physical body, because his mission was first and foremost in his focus. He often forgot to eat, and he slept very little. He was exhausted and had lost an extreme amount of weight.

Michael was all about love, and that was the message he wanted to share with everyone. "You are love," I said. "Yes, I am," he replied. "It is my message as well."

"Michael," I said, "you must remember how to use your wings. It is vital to your journey. There are things that you can do with them that can touch others profoundly. You can comfort people, heal people with them."

He said, "I am so tired, but I have to keep going."

"Yes, you do, but if you don't take time to regenerate, to replenish yourself, you won't make it."

"I know I just don't know what to do with this body. It is foreign to me in every way."

So I gave Michael suggestions about how to find balance in his situation, and how to ground himself so that he could function more safely and efficiently. There he was, an angel of perfection, bound in an imperfect body in an imperfect world, and the extent of his emotions were overwhelming him.

Toward the end of our conversation I asked him what he was going to do next. He suggested that he might wander elsewhere, and said something about going to Tibet, among other places. I encouraged Michael to call me regularly, but I never heard from him again. I still wonder. I hope he made it.

KARA

I visited Canada a couple of years ago to teach a workshop. While I was there, one of the attendees approached me about her 16-year-old daughter, whom I will call Kara. The girl had been very sick for many months, so the mother asked me if I had time to schedule a healing session with her daughter.

The day came for our session. It was at the end of the day, so we had no time limits or interruptions. When I stepped into the waiting area, my eyes immediately locked onto Kara. She exuded sadness: she was thin, with big black circles under her eyes—and she was beautiful. The sadness I felt was intertwined with some of the most unique energy that I had ever felt, yet the weight of her sadness felt to me as if she was drowning in it. Her life force was very weak. Mom was terrific, giving us plenty of space for conversation. At first Kara was not very open, as she didn't know me. In quick order, we established a "safe zone" in which to talk, and every moment that went by led to more and more ease between us.

Kara told me that she had wings, and that she had always been aware of them. She was frustrated that no one else could see them to validate her. She was living in multiple realities simultaneously, and there was no one available for her human side to reach out to for camaraderie or validation. Thus, the human side of Kara had moved into a cosmic depression. She didn't fit. No one could understand her.

"I have wings," she said.

"Yes," I said. "I can see them."

"They are so real for me that I had wings tattooed on my back so I can see them in the mirror. My wings are very blue." *How creative*, I thought.

In fact, her real wings were a powdery grayish-blue, and were lit from within, creating a subtle, transparent bluish glow around the edges. They appeared to be very fragile, but I knew they were not.

"I am afraid," she began tentatively.

I met her remark with attentive silence and a direct gaze that told her I was open to anything she had to say, and that there was nothing she could tell me that would be too strange. I validated Kara by telling her a little bit about my own strange gifts, and she continued to talk to me.

> I am afraid because I see everything—and worse, I feel everything too. I don't understand how to find balance with all of this. Everywhere I go I see others like me who don't realize who they are. I see angels, spirit guides, and the spirits of dead people. Dark entities follow me around, watching me all of the time. They aren't always the same, but I feel like they are after me in some way. Everywhere I go they follow me around. I see other realities blended over this one. It is very confusing to know what is "real" and what isn't. Worse, I don't remember how to protect myself. I don't have any energy. When I try to move, my body feels so heavy that it seems nearly impossible, but I keep trying. It is just that I have been sick for months now and I feel like I am at the end of my rope.

Kara meant it.

Take a deep breath, I said to myself. *We have a lot to do here.* Slowly and carefully I went back through some of what she had said. We talked of multidimensional realities, different kinds of energy, and how all of the beings she was seeing have a purpose in the whole of reality.

As we talked, I began to compare her gifts and experiences to some I have had, which are just as strange. I would point to an experience she was having and tell her, "If you know this, then you must have also seen that. If you have had this happen, then you also went through that." Her eyes widened with amazement. Someone else could relate to the things she was going through, and it was exciting to her. We talked for more than three hours, relating our etheric experiences back and forth to one another. Ultimately, Kara and I went into one of the healing rooms and worked together. Her energy field was velvety smooth, but had gotten chaotic and filled with static with all of her futile attempts to emotionally process her otherworldly experiences. As we worked, Kara became stronger and stronger. I reminded her how to protect herself, and explained to her that many of the beings she witnessed were merely curious. After all, an angel in the third dimension is a bit different!

Eventually I could see and feel balance moving through her energy fields. Because third-dimensional existence was so traumatic for her, Kara's energy field was very fragmented; her energy pathways were mixed and confused, following errant courses instead of their normal route. In spite of all of this, the most important thing was that Kara really wanted to be well. Most of all, she needed to know that she wasn't alone. She needed to know that her experiences were real and that having them was okay.

Slowly but surely, Kara's energy fields began to respond to the work we were doing together. I began to witness normalization on level after level of her entire energetic system. The energy leakage stopped, and her body began to revitalize. I knew that it would be just a matter of time before Kara's life would begin to normalize to the point that she would feel vital and healthy again. I remember thinking how grateful I felt to be able to share in Kara's healing. It was quite humbling to know that I had an angel quite literally in my hands. Before she left, I found the courage to ask to see her tattooed wings, and Kara obliged. There, covering her entire back, were two of the most artfully drawn wings I had ever seen—and they even had the color right! Armed with the fact that she wasn't crazy, Kara left that night with a new lease on life—merely because someone had taken the time to validate her experiences. That night she told her mom that I had talked to her about things that she had never confided to anyone, and that I just *knew*. She was very excited.

Over the next months, Kara healed and became strong. I heard from her mom that Kara has become very happy in general, and has even found a boyfriend!

As these stories demonstrate, there are times when angels enter our reality for great purpose, but become lost along the way. There are children in our world today who desperately need the same type of validation that Kara needed. In addition to the young angels who are described in this chapter, there are "adult" angels on Earth. Many of them live quietly among others, never tipping their hand. Others come forward in the form of teachers, mentors, healers, or a myriad of other human manifestations of subtle perfection.

When the divine meets the imperfection inherent in the human form (as it does with these angels on Earth), even mere existence becomes problematic. These stories may sound much like psychotic episodes, but I can assure the reader that these children are quite sane; they just need reinforcement and validation.

How Can
We Help?

CHAPTER 12

SOCIAL SOLUTIONS

The concept of gifted people in our world is not a new phenomenon. The difference is in the prevalence of giftedness, as more and more adults awaken to greater realities, and more and more children are born gifted beyond the existing culture and society deem as normal. We are people of greatness. We all come from the same source, the same perfection, but we forget that. If we are to honor our children, we need to nurture them as necessary so that future gifted generations will grow up to have the strength, courage, wisdom, and personal power to work for the greater good of humanity. We must recognize them now.

In order to create wondrous and positive changes in our world, the first step is to admit the truth of these children. We must not let our egos or our ignorance stand in the way. The Children of Now are the teachers of greater reality. Can we accept that? We must! Secondly, we must disseminate this information so that it reaches the mainstream of people around the globe, as this phenomenon is not limited geographically. So far, there are a few books and movies that address the Children of Now, but they have barely scratched the surface. These kids are not anomalies to be put on display or sensationalized. They are real people with real feelings, who just happen to have heightened awareness and amazing perceptions of our world and beyond.

Instead of seeing our gifted children as different or flawed, and instead of allowing them to fall through the cracks just because they don't fit our perceptions, we must embrace them, nurture them, and encourage them to share their gifts with us. Just because they are differently able doesn't mean there is anything wrong with them. Quite the contrary. Time after time I meet children who have been dragged to this doctor or that psychiatrist and a myriad of other professionals, as the parents try to understand and "fix" them. The doctors can't find anything wrong with the kids, but the problems persist behaviorally, in their school grades, in their relationships, and in life in general. *There is nothing wrong with these kids.* They just know more and remember more, but no one is listening to them. A multidimensionally aware child who thinks compartmentally and holographically cannot sit still in a chair for any length of time. It is impossible! So let's look at some solutions for how to surround these beautiful children in love and support so that they can become all they are meant to be.

First of all, we must ACT. That means to embrace:
Awareness
Communication
Truth

We have to create awareness socially, at home, and in our schools that, yes, some children are different, and that's okay. Think of John Everett's mom, who took an Indigo book to every one of her son's teachers and the principal of his school. She wanted to make sure they understood her son. Also, we must not be afraid to talk about things that we don't understand. There is a lot going on in our world that we don't comprehend, but that is not a problem in and of itself. The problem is found in inaction, and in the attitude that someone else will figure it all out. In the meantime, countless children are being disregarded who could have otherwise shone light on the very answers we need. Talk about this! Above all, we must tell the truth to our kids, our families, our friends, and everyone else who touches our children's lives. Ideally, no matter what our belief systems dictate, if our child tells us that there is an angel present, you can bet it is there. If our child speaks profoundly or seems to have a different view than we do, so be it. If our child tells us that there are other people present, and even goes on to name them, there is a great possibility that this is so. If our children become quiet or sick, and we can't figure out why, perhaps we are looking in the wrong direction. Perhaps they are not getting what they need, or are too stressed from things that are happening in their home or school environments. If our children tell us what they remember from before they were our children, let's not contradict them; let's ask them for more details and allow them to share unresolved feelings and memories. Children don't know how to make up these kinds of stories, particularly when they are so detailed. We teach them to be untruthful when we tell them that their perceptions, experiences, and memories aren't real. When

198 THE CHILDREN OF NOW

they ask us to explain things that even we as adults don't understand, let us be truthful, answering their questions thoughtfully and truthfully to the best of our abilities. Let us nurture their hearts, souls, minds, and bodies. Let us show them that the love they feel and express is not in vain.

We cannot let our lack of understanding get in the way of true giftedness. We must honor our children. Remember Sky, who quit telling people what she knows because they laughed at her? It was the general public that made a show of a heavenly and sincere child. What a shame, what a loss. Let us admit that we have something really important happening in our world—namely, our children, the changes they bring, and the possibilities they freely offer to us.

HEALING THE GENERATIONS

While they are often gifted beyond comprehension, the Children of Now are not spectacles. They are not circus acts. They are vastly evolved human beings with sacred messages—reminders of who we are and where we are going. To put them on a pedestal accomplishes very little except to train their egos to crave attention. We cannot live vicariously through any of our children. When children learn to grab attention using their gifts, the medium becomes more important than the message, and the truth becomes diluted. Time and again I have met families of gifted children in which the dynamics have degenerated to the point that the kids are running the entire household. In these situations, they often become demanding, even making derogatory comments to or about their parents and others. They become bossy and out of control. Because the children seem to know so much and seem wise beyond their years, parents and others often put these kids on a pedestal. They let the children reign without boundaries or any kind of structure. So, the child who began as a gift to the world suddenly becomes self-centered and attention-seeking. Allowing these kids to "run the show" creates little ones who will grow up to be rude and self-centered adults. Not at all what we meant for them!

Remember what Nicholas wrote in his foreword? *Although my cosmic adventures have taken me all the way, from walking beside Jesus to Atlantis, here I am "all-knowing" and innocent at the same time. You see, we the Crystalline and Star Children may appear all-capable, yet we require the world's capacity for deep listening to resolve in our purpose and best effect change.* What wise words from one of our brilliantly gifted children! To the children, their giftedness is their reality, their norm. It is only society that stigmatizes our children and labels them as different. Nicholas recognizes that the children may be all-knowing, but they are still children who need guidance and structure in order to accomplish what they have come to do. We must give them some sort of structure or boundaries so that they know what to expect and can learn to function in this world. We must also encourage their giftedness in constructive ways. For instance, instead of making a spectacle of your child by telling everyone who will listen about a fantastic experience he or she had, or some profound thing that he or she said, why not ask the child gently and sincerely if he or she has any more insight on the subject. Get your child to verbalize his or her experiences without the drama and without the sensationalism. I also highly suggest keeping a journal, as some of the insights the children share are quite profound yet easily forgotten over time. Ask your child open-ended questions about his or her experiences, rather than "yes or no" questions—but most of all, *listen to them* as they answer. We are often so busy that we only half listen to our children as we rush into whatever is next. Ask them heartfelt questions, and answer their questions with the same attitude of mindfulness and respect.

Drama is destructive in that it maintains a certain level of chaos in the home. I call that "drama and trauma," because you can't have one without the other. When drama is high, no one is listening and everyone is reacting; nothing gets figured out or settled, only exacerbated. Chaos reigns. Instead, why not look at situations with our children from a mature point of view? Why not break our old family patterns and allow ourselves to heal the dysfunction that we may have been given? Why not give our gifted new generation a healthier set of tools that they can take into the world to effect change?

If we are to give our children every opportunity to fulfill who they are, we as parents, caregivers, teachers, and friends must first begin to heal our bodies, minds, and spirits, and that requires honesty and integrity. If we cannot be honest with ourselves, how can we be honest with anyone else, especially our children? Self-healing also entails looking deeply within ourselves to find out why we constantly recreate the same types of situations, and why we remain in those patterns that keep us in turmoil. What is it that we are trying to learn? Why do we allow fear to control us? For example, time and again we might find ourselves in a situation in which we give and give, until someone takes advantage of our generosity—to the point that our desires are disregarded and our feelings are hurt. When we give without having learned to receive, it is generally indicative that we are afraid of rejection, or of not being liked or loved. Our giving assures us that we will be valued, but what we are really doing is covering our fear of not being good enough.

Recognizing these patterns of behavior is the first step toward healing them. Once we have recognized that we are stuck in those patterns, and once we realize that living those patterns is a choice, we can choose differently! I don't believe that we must relive every moment of our painful past experiences in order to heal ourselves. Instead, if we can get to the bottom of what drives us in those circumstances, we can heal ourselves almost instantly— when we are willing. As we become stronger and healthier people, that strength, that healthfulness, is what we will pass on to our children. Perhaps most of all, we must learn to recognize our perfection. We must remember that everything that we need is already within us. We are mighty and powerful beings! And that is precisely what we must demonstrate to our children.

COMMUNICATION

Communication is vital, but it must be balanced. Although the children are wise beyond their years, they are still not adults in this world. With their profound words and actions, it is often easy to forget that they are still children. By the same token, however, we cannot talk to the Children of Now as if they are babies. In fact, in this writer's humble opinion, talking to babies as if they are unintelligent does not help them grow; rather, it actually delays their progress.

Conversely, there are some parents who make the mistake of pressuring their children to perform because of their brilliance. Unfortunately, these parents are operating from the vantage point of old paradigms that no longer serve our world. These paradigms have bred neediness and feelings of emptiness in many people. We can't live vicariously through our children; it is time to move out into the world from a place of fullness and strength. We must let the brilliance of these kids guide their journeys. They really do know what they are doing. We must honor their accomplishments, no matter how large or small, and respect their feelings and perceptions, knowing that they feel them to their very core.

The Children of Now require honest, open conversation, in which we talk not only with our words, but with our actions and energies. The children take all of this into consideration when interpreting our messages to them. They know unequivocally where the truth lies, even when we don't. Do our words and our actions match, or do we say one thing then do another? What does our body language say to our children? Do we face them eye-to-eye and heart-to-heart with honesty? Or do we fling answers or demands at them as we rush through the room? Do we communicate fully, or do we just say what we have to because we are busy with life? Do we really listen to the children, or just patronize them and go on with our business? Do we notice the look in their eyes, and the nuances in their words and posture? What are they really telling us?

We must listen to the Children of Now, because their messages are vital to humanity. As Nicholas points out, when the children have the benefit of deep listening, they are able to experience full relaxation. This relaxation is not simply of the body—it is a calming of the spirit within. As we listen deeply, it is also important to tell the children the truth no matter what, and to encourage their giftedness, ask their opinions, and open greater communication. We must be fully present with these wise souls, slowing down long enough to completely experience them.

The Children of Now need to be nurtured. There is a great difference between nurturing and spoiling a child. To nurture a child means to hold them, love them, and communicate with them, and open our hearts to what they have to say to us. It means to give them more than just their basic needs. It means to give them the emotional, spiritual, mental, and physical tools they need to stay balanced within. That means stopping our old patterns that don't work anymore. It means that honesty must be paramount. It means becoming consciously creative within our own lives as well as those of our children. This does *not* mean we should treat them as if they were tiny adults; it just means to pay attention and treat them as we would want to be treated. Nurturing the children also does not mean buying every popular toy for them or filling their life with things. It means sharing their lives from the heart.

More than ever before, our children need guidance. When children are gifted, they give the impression that they have a handle on everything. Although they are wise enough to consider their options and make mature choices in certain situations, they are still children, and they are not old enough to make life decisions without guidance. We can help by offering explanations, options, and information, as well as guidance and structure. Some of the greatest dysfunction I have seen in older kids comes from parents who gave the kids full rein in their decision-making process, without enough adult guidance to go with that freedom. Those children often become overwhelmed and unsure, and slow in making decisions. Sometimes they simply choose not to decide at all. They become paralyzed and stuck. We need to guide our children responsibly while allowing them to learn how to make good decisions. For instance, when a child must make a choice in life, we can help him or her explore the possible outcomes of various decisions. By talking through each scenario, he or she will learn to look at life situations from all sides. The child then learns to approach future decisions from a thoughtful perspective, rather than out of a desire for immediate gratification. This process also stresses how decisions can affect other people or future situations. Thus, the child will learn to make informed decisions—and hopefully good choices.

We must speak the truth and act the truth, because the children know when we don't. Drama and overreaction are greatly discouraged, because these kids feel everything. With calmer communication dynamics, and if given half the chance, most of these kids are quite willing to look at all aspects of a situation. Most parents and caregivers who implement this type of communication generally find that, ultimately, the children are teaching them!

HOME ENVIRONMENTS

As we discussed earlier, the Children of Now are extremely environmentally sensitive. The environment pertains not only to the quality of the air we breathe, the land we occupy, and the water we drink, but also to the surroundings in our homes and our schools. Indeed, it is everywhere we go. Environment is also about aesthetics; how our environment looks and feels has everything to do with how comfortable we are there. Because the energy fields of the Children of Now are comprised of light frequencies that have higher vibrations than those of previous generations, extra care must be taken in the creation of their environments. The energy fields of these kids are more sensitive than our skin. They actually *feel* color, light, sound, and even shapes, just as we feel things tactilely. But for these children, it is as if someone turned up the volume receptor in their sensitivity. This heightened sense of feeling actually extends, antennae–like, many feet from their bodies. When the energy field of a sensitive child is touched by vibrations of color, sound, shapes, or other input, the child feels that input to his or her core. If an environment is uncomfortable, a child will often become overstimulated and act out. Although this hypersensitivity probably does not register on a conscious level, the child's inability to verbalize his or her subconscious discomfort creates a "felt" distress, which then shows up in his or her moods and behaviors.

The children's moods and comfort levels are easily affected by the colors in their surroundings. Soft, cheerful colors—such as pastels in blues, pinks, greens, teals, and lavenders—are optimal for a calm environment. Care should be taken to stay away from bright yellows and reds, because a child in a very yellow or red environment is more likely to be anxious, nervous, or hyperactive. This is because color is frequency, and frequency (as energy) is sound and movement. The energy of color interacts with, and actually changes, our personal energy systems. Dark colors, such as deep browns, blues, greens, or purples, have slower frequencies, and thus are probably too grounding for sensitive kids. To a sensitive child (or even an adult), these heavy dark colors can actually feel like a weight dragging them down. If a sensitive child spends large amounts of time in rooms with these dark colors, he or she will ultimately begin to show signs of "the blues," or even mild to moderate depression. If, for aesthetics, a choice is made to combine certain colors in a room or home, care must be taken to choose colors that are in similar frequencies. For example, you shouldn't mix navy blue and teal, lime green and red, or any colors that are disharmonic with each other.

Aural (hearing) and visual inputs are extremely important as well. Too much sound and/or too much in the visual field can cause these children to become uncomfortable or overloaded. The noise of a TV, radio, video games, or even constant talking will escalate negative behaviors, so it is a good idea to limit the volume level of any electronics, as well as the time allowed for using them. Rooms filled with disorder or disarray, or even walls with lots of posters and pictures and little clean space, can be disturbing or overstimulating as well. Clean surfaces are conducive to calmer kids. Bookshelves that are organized by size; pictures on walls that are accents instead of just "filler"; solid-colored furniture that is coordinated with the rest of the room; and general order with specific places for toys and craft supplies (perhaps inexpensive organizational space savers with drawers and shelves that can be found at most home improvement stores) are all good examples of how to go about changing the cluttered environment. Because the Children of Now are "hard-wired" to nature, live plants, garden projects, and even running water—in the form of fountains or fish tanks—are more excellent ways to create a comfortable and soothing environment.

Basic geometric shapes add an amazing dimension to the overall energy of a room. Spheres, pyramids (four-sided), cubes, octahedrons, and so on are basic energy forms that are found in all of creation. There are inherent memories within all of us that recognize these basic shapes and resonate harmonically with them. Geometric shapes are also easy to keep clean!

Another thing to keep in mind is that EMF waves (electromagnetic frequencies) can interfere with the children's energy fields, causing them to rearrange into disharmonic patterns. EMF interference can come from a variety of sources, including TVs, computers, power lines, microwave ovens, video games, and so on. Any of these can cause behavioral issues or drain a child's physical energy.

ACTIVITIES

Because the Children of Now think compartmentally, activities of a linear format do not serve anyone well for long. The compartmental thinker multitasks as a matter of course, so it is natural for the Children of Now to direct their attention in many directions at once. What appears to be a limited attention span is actually the ability to keep track of many things at the same time. These children are like sponges, absorbing everything around them. They can change gears mentally in seamless fashion. For instance, they will talk about their art project one moment and multidimensional reality the next—seemingly out of the blue. Or they will go from petting the dog to talking about quantum mechanics and back again. At times, this can be a bit unnerving to parents or caregivers who are unfamiliar with the phenomenon! The best way to deal with this type of behavior is to provide multiple choices of activities simultaneously. Up to five different activities is optimal. For example, for a young child, a coloring book and crayons; paper and paint; flash cards with letters, numbers, or words; a board game; and perhaps a craft of some kind are all good possibilities. The activities are all interesting to the child as well, so play is interspersed with learning. Remember to change the activities regularly to maintain the child's interest.

The Children of Now tend to leave trails of their activities from one room to another, so certain ground rules must apply. Each activity should have its own location that is acceptable to the parent, such as a table where spilled paint won't be a problem. The activity must remain in the designated area. The child may go from one activity to another at his or her leisure, but is responsible for cleaning up and organizing his or her mess. The child must be required to finish whatever projects are started prior to cleanup time. This approach should alleviate those trails of activities, and relieve tired parents of constantly having to clean up after their kids. This approach also works well if there is more than one child, as having a choice of activities makes it more likely that the children will share with each other. Occupying children in multitasking that is fun and constructive feeds their incessant creative curiosity, and gives them outlets for their high energy flows. This results in calmer children, and calmer households in general.

For parents with Star Children, field trips to planetariums or science centers are a fantastic way to feed their scientific leanings. Erector sets, models with moving parts or motors, chemistry sets (with supervision, of course), crystal-growing kits, bug farms, radio-building kits—really, anything that has some technical value—are all good choices. Of course, books are always welcome! Field trips to parks, nature trails, or zoos (where the children can interact with animals) are also great.

Above all, gentle yet consistent structure is vital to these kids. They need to know what to expect and what is expected of them. If the children have no idea what success looks like, they will not succeed. If they don't have a clear understanding of the rules, they cannot comply. Clear communication of what is expected and consistent follow-up is a must. The Children of Now are very comfortable when they know their parameters. To this end, praise for success is paramount for successful accomplishment. Also, instead of punishing right off the bat, parents must discuss their children's indiscretions with them so that they know exactly why and how they haven't complied with the rules. For example, if a child disobeys a rule of the home, you might begin the conversation by asking the child to explain how he or she broke the rule. This creates awareness. Next, you could ask the child how he or she could change that behavior next time in order to make a different choice. Make sure you give the child time to answer thoughtfully! Doing this helps the child learn how to make positive and effective choices. Finally, ask the child if he or she has learned anything from the situation, and be prepared to discuss this with the child's point of view in mind. In many cases, I have found that the child simply had a different view of what was right in that moment and thus meant no harm, so flexibility and patience are important. A willingness to listen to the child, as well as communicate the rules, is part of the remedy. Simply barking rules to the Children of Now—or any child, for that matter—is not conducive to success and harmony within the family. The children know what is right and wrong, and they generally have a greater sense of integrity about this than do most adults. Essentially, parents must be willing to consider their child's point of view. Sometimes their different perceptions can amaze and delight, or provoke deeper discussion and awareness all the way around.

CONNECTIONS

Many of the parents with whom I have spoken feel very isolated in their situations. They have children who display amazing gifts—and who may or may not look or act like "normal" kids—and there just aren't enough opportunities for them to meet other parents and children in similar situations. Some families, because their children are very different mentally or physically, find themselves more and more alone. Finances are sometimes tight because of medical expenses or the large amounts of time the parents have been required to spend with their children. This makes travel difficult or even impossible. The families I have gotten to know live all over the country—indeed, all over the world. They feel separate from society, even though their children are some of the greatest examples of humanity.

I would like to see a network developed that would include a communications forum for parents and children. This could involve the Internet, hotlines manned by parents, and social gatherings—all of which would allow families and caregivers to get together and meet others who are in similar circumstances. (The Website, *www.childrenofthenewearth.com*, plans expansion toward these very goals. It also hosts forums that allow parents and children to talk to each other online.) Perhaps we could even develop a scholarship system that raises funds for families to travel to these types of activities. Once there, parents, teachers, children, and others could take center stage and share their stories and messages to the world. This could be put together as a yearly or biannual conference, a symposium of gifted beings and those who support them. Of course, this would have to be done in a way that is affordable. All too often, conferences or gatherings begin with good intent and later end up being out of balance, with professionals clamoring to present to the group, and families only getting the chance to talk in the hallway between lectures. Situations that are more interactive would be of the highest benefit for everyone. Perhaps some of the "experts" in the field would donate their services free of charge. This author would! Another possibility is a camp, where parents and kids could go to share and learn from each other, and gifted children could find their true peers. There would be activities geared toward exercising the children's gifts and expanding them to greater use.

Internet chat rooms or message boards are other easy solutions to enable parents, teachers, and caregivers to compare notes. I recently heard of one chat room in Wisconsin where a group of the Children of Now have come together to talk about their gifts and awareness. (Of course, any time kids are online they should be supervised, as there are very real predators our there who monitor and even participate in children's chat rooms.) The whole point is to put a stop to the perception that gifted children are anomalies. The Children of Now are everywhere and are vital to human evolution, so we must make room for our perceived differences and assist the children in whatever ways we can.

SUGGESTIONS FOR DIETARY CHANGES

This writer is admittedly not a dietary expert. The information in this section has been gained from interviews with parents and professionals who have found these suggestions helpful, as well as from good old-fashioned common sense.

Because our DNA relationships are continually evolving—and will ultimately change completely—the kind of information our bodies receive also changes. The absolute best way to assure that the Children of Now meet their dietary needs would be to tailor their diets according to their individual DNA. If our children's diets were planned based upon their DNA, they would be constantly changing as their energy fields evolved. They would receive optimal sustenance all of the time. Imagine—continuously evolving, state-of-the-art nutrition! Of course, this technology is not entirely practical, and is not yet generally available to the public. Someday!

In our chaotic world, there never seems to be enough time to do all of the things that we need to do. We have become people of convenience, and with that has come poor diet. Many of us tend to eat on the fly, and we feed our children the same way. Institutionally prepared foods that are microwavable or expedient usually contain all kinds of preservatives, and they often barely resemble their natural state. Naturally prepared foods have become more and more readily available, and while they may cost an extra dollar or two, the benefit they offer to our bodies is priceless. It takes just a little more time to prepare fresh vegetables than it does to open a can and pour it into a pot. Vegetables that are commercially packaged are already cooked and in that process have lost a lot of their nutrients. Just because something is offered to us in a grocery store does not mean that the product is healthy or good for us. Marketing hype causes many of us to eat things that really aren't good for us, but we believe that they are because of the labels that scream "healthy food here." As with anything, parents should use their discretion regarding their children's dietary needs. The Children of Now are generally very good at listening to their bodies, and they seem to know what they need. Usually, when given the opportunity, they will make surprisingly healthy choices. Young children in particular seem to be highly aware of their needs, so listening to them rather than just going for convenience is a great idea.

The Children of Now have metabolic systems that require their bodies to be fed differently, particularly the Crystalline Children. They need to eat very often in small amounts, rather than heavy meals three times a day. The Crystallines and some of the Star Kids—particularly the smaller children—would rather eat like birds. This doesn't mean we should hand them a carrot and let them run around playing while they eat. Instead, thoughtful preparation of meals and snacks goes a long way. (If anyone reading this has or knows of a gifted child, you have probably witnessed the dinnertime challenge of a child who isn't interested in eating. The child will pick at his or her food, not really wanting it. How many of us have heard, "How many more bites?" from a child? Granted, there are some kids who just don't want to have their play interrupted, but that is not what we are talking about here. Because the Children of Now are extremely sensitive, perhaps we should consider the possibility that they might be miserable with the idea of having to eat something that doesn't resonate with them.

When kids do not eat in a beneficial manner, they do not function optimally. The New Kids are particularly vulnerable to reactions to food because, like everything else, food is energy, and each kind of food has a vibration all its own. I received an e-mail recently from a woman who was amazed at her Crystalline niece's ability to determine what kinds of foods or drinks she needed. In one instance, the child's mom had offered her some juice that was a blend of several different types. The child carefully considered her choice and then chose a different blend that did not have a particular fruit in it. This wasn't a matter of taste, but of somehow knowing her needs. Another example is the grandmother who took her two grandchildren to a Whole Foods grocery store. Usually their mother takes them to the grocery store and allows them to have a wide variety of institutionally prepared food and lots of junk food—candies, cookies, and other prepared snacks. As the grandmother took the kids up and down the aisles, she was stunned to see that, with little to no guidance from her, the children picked out fresh food—fresh vegetables, fruits, juices, nuts. You name it, it went in the basket. The children had no education regarding their diets, yet left to choose, they chose wisely. Brand name was not an issue for the kids, and it was obvious they were shopping from their inner guidance.

If your child or one you know consistently has dark circles under his or her eyes, digestive issues, or other symptoms such as lack of energy, it might be a good idea to have them checked for food sensitivities. Food sensitivities can create toxicity within the body, which in turn may cause an array of problems that range from mild to more severe. Over time, the body may become stressed or overworked as it tries to compensate for the toxicity. Because of this, care should be taken to avoid foods that may have residual hormones or antibiotics (such as meat, eggs, and milk), unless they are free-range or organically produced. Foods that are genetically altered should also be avoided. The scientific community is not taking into consideration that whenever they genetically modify our foods, they change the way those foods are assimilated into our bodies. Ultimately, if genetic alteration continues, the way in which our cells relate to different molecules in our bodies will change. Different protein relationships will be created, which will affect how we assimilate our food and nutrients, and thus how we function as biological organisms. These changes will become part of our evolution. If this is allowed to continue unchecked, this will eventually affect the entire food chain, which could cause mutations in our plants, our animals, and even us.

Our bodies are about 80 percent water. As we burn calories and as energy moves through our bodies, much of that water evaporates. It is important for us to remain hydrated. The Crystalline Children in particular require huge amounts of liquids. Many of them seem to have a thirst that is incessant. Because of their high metabolic rates, and because they are conduits for energy, they burn up their fluid intake rapidly. Star Children require a lot of liquids as well, but seem to go longer between refills. In addition to water, fruit or vegetable juices, milk (organic whenever available), sports drinks that replace electrolytes (in moderation), and other natural drinks are all good choices to help kids stay hydrated.

Sugar should be avoided, because the New Kids easily go into "hyperdrive" with even small amounts of it. Sugar temporarily reverses the polarities, or electrical charges, within our nervous systems, right down to the minutest aspects. This causes excitement of the tiny subatomic particles within our body. Because of this effect, we temporarily feel "up," and later tired, because our bodies have had to overwork to compensate for the sugar intake. Because our nervous system is the communication system of our body, we must treat it with respect and not force it to overwork. If we absolutely must have sugar, raw sugar is now available in most groceries. This sugar consists of large granules that are light brown in color. It is actually very good. Another good substitute for refined sugar is stevia, a food additive derived from a subtropical plant in the sunflower family. This can be found primarily in health food stores, in either liquid or powdered form.

Instead of junk food, snacks can consist of fresh fruits, such as apples and oranges, natural fruit roll-ups (also called "fruit leather"), or other similar products. Peanut butter and celery, cream cheese on crackers or celery, or vegetables with homemade dip are great too. It doesn't take much imagination to supply healthy snacks for children, just a little extra time. How foods are combined is also important. Believe it or not, the body requires different enzymes for different digestive tasks. It takes one kind of enzyme to digest meat, another for fruit, another for dairy, and so on. When foods that are digestively incompatible are served at the same time, the result is less-than-adequate digestion, which in turn can lead to an array of problems—one of the most common being weight gain. It is also a good idea to limit simple carbohydrates in the kid's diets. It is best to stay away from breads that contain chemical preservatives; as long as the child doesn't have gluten or wheat sensitivity, stay with whole grain breads instead. Avoiding partially hydrogenated fats is also highly recommended. These stay in the system about four times longer than regular fats, which are a natural and beneficial part of the human diet. Low-fat foods are not necessarily healthy!

Supplemental nutrition can also be very helpful to the children. The most frequent piece of advice I have received from parents, teachers, and caregivers about sustaining the Children of Now nutritionally is to support the children's immune systems. Fish oils rich in omega-3 fatty acids; vitamin C in the form of citrus fruits (assists in clarification and cleansing of the lymphatic system, and refines the electromagnetic conductivity within the body); vitamins E, A, and D; garlic; and a good multivitamin with minerals are all good choices. Dark, leafy-green vegetables (such spinach and kale) all contain properties that enhance health, and can even help prevent cancer. Of course, it is always a good idea to consult a physician before starting a child on any diet or vitamin regimen. The bottom line here is to use common sense, observe the effects of what our children eat, and have a great deal of flexibility regarding our children's nutritional needs and desires.

SOLUTIONS *at* SCHOOL

CHAPTER 13

ENHANCING THE SCHOOL EXPERIENCE

Besides the home environment, one of the most important arenas in which society can impact the lives of the Children of Now is in the school systems. Nurturing the whole being of the children—body, mind, and spirit—is vitally important to their growth and to the fullness of their learning processes. Presently, however, we are feeding the minds of the children, but not their souls. Day after day we provide school environments that wear them down until, in an effort to maintain some functionality within the environment, the children stray or become apathetic and numb. Many of the kids become sick with illnesses that don't seem to have a particular organic cause. (These and the following observations can be applied to many "normal" kids as well.)

The Children of Now are so sensitive that the stark and often chaotic institutional environments in our public and private schools make them very uncomfortable. To these kids, chaos is literally painful. Rooms filled with children of all different backgrounds and attitudes make it difficult for them to adapt and thrive. The clutter and chaos in the typical school environment is just the beginning of the problem, however. Institutional and overly regimented environments are detrimental as well. Hard corners, rough surfaces, and too much visual or audio input are all like fingernails on a blackboard to these kids. Fluorescent lighting is harsh and causes eye problems and headaches in some of the New Kids. All of this, plus EMF emissions from ceiling lights, computers, and other equipment in the schools can drain necessary energy. Throw in general misbehavior from some of the kids, or a teacher having a bad day, and the Children of Now just can't handle it like other children. Each of the subgroups of these kids tends to handle these situations differently: Crystalline Children feel it all right to the core, and will want to "fix" everything so that everyone is happy—a huge job for little kids! Star Children, on the other hand, will most likely zone out in a book, or something else that interests them intellectually, and ignore everyone. (Many of the Star Kids internalize their feelings, and this can be quite damaging to them in the long run.) The Transitional Kids will either come up with fantastic ways to make a difference, or they will call attention to the situation in a less-than-acceptable way. Still others of this group will move completely into negative behavior.

The school systems have become so overcrowded, understaffed, and underbudgeted, that even the teachers have a difficult time performing optimally. Add to that a combination of children from different homes, cultures, and socio-economic environments, and what naturally develops is a clique system amongst the kids, indifference amongst much of the staff, and a school system that is much less than successful in reaching all of the children. As the children attempt to survive in the face of what looks like an insurmountable challenge, outlooks become bleak, and violence often becomes prevalent. The end result of all of this has become an uneducated and ignorant public, unaware not only of academics, but of larger world issues and events as well. We have become a nation of sheep that are being led and fed by politicians and the media. We have been conditioned to accept the ideas and ideals of others as they are served to us on a platter, and this is leading our world into great divisiveness in the form of violence, wars, and the decline of culture among the masses.

Much of this begins in our schools. *It is time for great change.* It is time to nurture our children, and time to change attitudes if our society is to evolve into one that will benefit the whole. When we nurture today's children by implementing new (and more beneficial) environments, and embracing diverse methods of teaching, we will begin to see a reflection of our social consciousness in their eyes. The children will become strong individuals, and they will apply that strength and their giftedness to everything they do.

Time and again I have heard how special children and kids with special needs are asked to leave one school after another. Apparently there is a general lack of skill and training in "mainstreaming" kids who are different. This goes for physical disabilities as well as other more subtle differences, some of which have been outlined in this book. When these differences are not nurtured, it is a disservice not only to the children, but to their families, the community, and future generations as well. The bottom line is that the current public and even private school environments and attitudes are not conducive to the well-being of these delightfully sensitive and gifted kids.

I recently heard of a little girl in a Georgia public school who is psychically gifted. She is, I am told, about 6 years old. She is a Crystalline Child. This little one was reading palms on the playground, innocently using her intuitive gifts. For that she was expelled from school—as a witch! Yes, in the 21st century and in the United States, people were afraid of her differences! She is the second child who I have heard about recently who has been ostracized because she is differently gifted. The first one was suspended for three days for a similar situation.

How to deal with all of this in a world where schools are underfunded, understaffed, and overcrowded?

In order to best describe the changes that are needed in our schools, I thought it would be most appropriate to hear from one of our special kids regarding his own personal experience:

> In my own personal experience attending a special school, I was treated as though I was invisible. It did not have to do with my physical body as much as my Crystalline traits. Every day as my mommy drove me to school, I listened to the most beautiful soulful affirmation songs, yet when I arrived at school, those affirmations quickly dispersed.
>
> I became invisible in their eyes. I think they could sense my deep consciousness and they just weren't ready. So instead of listening to me

and my hurt feelings, they sent me out of the
classroom into the "Hall Hang-Out," where I
began to roar in my pain. If only they could
listen, I thought to myself, if only they could
take a moment to listen in, hear my wholeness,
and not ask [me] to separate myself into distant
parts. This annihilation of the parts, a shattering
of the whole, is the road we tend to go down as
Crystalline Children when we are not
experienced as whole.

I believe the question of school can be a
momentous time with many careful decisions,
yet when Spirit is in the driver's seat and the
families of Crystalline Children are in the
passenger seats, through watchful observance and
deep listening, a relaxation takes place. This is
the awakening of Spirit in all of us. This is the
universe knowing it is being listened to. This is
each Crystalline child responding with joy, and
celebrating the co-creation with Spirit. I must
emphasize deep listening is the key to a
relaxation of this whole situation.

> Bringer of Light and Love,
> Nicholas M. Tschense, 9 years

Nicholas's description of the annihilation of his parts
hit me hard. He reveals the typical Crystalline point of
view that everything and everyone is part of a greater
whole; when this is disregarded, the oneness they embody
is shattered, and that is painful to their core. How many of
these kids are out there day after day feeling the same way,
and who are not as eloquent as Nicholas in their ability to
share their feelings? Many of the kids just become quiet,
hang their heads, and coast through their days until they
can do something more comfortable.

HOMESCHOOLING

As a remedy to this situation, numbers of aware parents have taken matters in their own hands and started homeschooling their kids. Homeschooling allows for flexibility in scheduling, and allows students to learn at a pace that is comfortable for them. Some kids excel and need much less time to learn, and can easily succeed in a homeschool environment. Others who require more attention and assistance can receive it easily and without the stigma of being a little bit slower than others in some subjects.

There is a grassroots movement of families who have gotten very creative about their children's homeschooling education. From what I have been able to ascertain, the most successful are the families who gear their child's education around his or her passions. The children who are being nurtured in this way are not only adapting well, but excelling. Of course, the parents don't limit the subject matter only to this passion (which could be music, art, or science), but instead create inventive ways for the children to pursue their interests—for example, lessons to play an instrument or instruments; and field trips to art galleries, science centers, or other points of interest that involve the things in which the child is interested. As part of one child's education, her parents, who own a farm in Kansas, allowed her to grow a field of sunflowers. It was magnificent and quickly became a local attraction. The beautiful, blond-haired, blue-eyed creature had been fascinated with sunflowers, and as she brought her project to fruition, she learned the entire farming process—from planting to harvesting and everything in between. This girl also raises her own calves, bottle-feeding them and caring for them, and plays five different musical instruments. She speaks like an authority about almost everything because she has been encouraged to express her feelings and ideas. Other families are following suit, making a concerted effort to provide a well-rounded curriculum so that the children receive a full education.

Socialization is another thing to keep in mind when considering homeschooling. In some cases, homeschooling can isolate the child, and even the entire family. Interacting with other children and adults is a vital part of learning social skills, as well as learning to process feelings and experiences. As a solution to this, families in many areas are forming coalitions that enable homeschooled children to gather for field trips and social events. Some have their own Girl and Boy Scout troops as well. In other such groups, field trips and the like are typically done in much smaller, more intimate groups, and with more quality attention and experience. Overall, this type of situation appears to be working very well.

MAINSTREAM AND PRIVATE SCHOOL ENVIRONMENTS

In mainstream as well as private schools, changing the environment and the structure of each day can make a huge difference in the outcome of children's learning experiences, as well as in their behaviors. As we have learned, the Children of Now are extremely sensitive to their environments and to the feelings and actions of others. The first thing to do is to recreate the learning environment. Think about this: When we go to a school or some other institution, what does it look like to us? How does it feel? Are the walls institutional green or gray? Are the floors hard and cold? Is the general atmosphere of the building one that screams "low budget" and "rigid rules"? Are we intimidated by our surroundings? If so, why is this the case? It is because the "rhetoric" of certain kinds of environments implies unbending rules, unwavering authority, and tactile insult. Sometimes they don't feel very clean either. The paint is marred, the lighting is too bright, and the furniture is uncomfortable and old. Moreover, there are sharp angles everywhere, and there are few signs of natural life, such as plants or animals. This generally leaves people with a hollow feeling about the place. Paradoxically, the environment is uninteresting and creatively uninspiring, while it is overstimulating with its level of visual and aural clutter.

Imagine how our children feel, gifted or not, when they are made to sit in desks or chairs that are hard and uncomfortable. Generally they are arranged in rows with assigned seats, or are set up by the students by force of habit. Everyone is made to find a space that identifies them, and the children are conditionally trained to jump from that space as soon as the bell rings, finished or not.

LIGHT, SOUND, AND COLOR

Let's begin with the environment. First, the staff and children would be better served with indirect, natural lighting that does not emit EMF fields as strong or as wide as those from fluorescent lighting. EMF emissions affect everyone to some degree, but the Children of Now feel the emissions as palpable energy fields that intrude into their bodies and make them feel sick. EMF emissions rearrange the harmonic alignment of the particles within our energy fields, and when that occurs, the energy relationships in and around the body change, often with detrimental effects upon the children. The Crystalline Children in particular are extremely affected by EMF emissions, and many of them suffer fatigue and headaches from harsh classroom lighting. Other electronics, such as computers and monitors, are also detrimental to human energy fields, and therefore to the health of these kids. EMF emissions in the classroom can be reduced by changing the computer monitors from the old CRT type to the newer flat panel monitors. The flat panel monitors emit much lower measurable EMF pollution. (EMF emissions can be easily monitored with an inexpensive handheld meter.)

Another factor that affects both the attention span and the overall comfort of these children is something that I call visual and aural overload. This type of "sensory insult" occurs when there is so much in the visual field that it creates an inner sense of chaos, or when there is so much noise that it becomes overwhelming. Think of it this way: when someone has the TV on too loud, we can only take it so long before we have to ask for the noise to be turned down. In school, there is constant interruption from background noise in the classroom and in the hallways, as well as from noise coming from outside the windows, and these distractions affect the ability of most children to concentrate. And in an institution at work, it seems that there is just too much to turn down.

Simplifying the environmental, visual, and aural experience will contribute greatly to the comfort of all children. This can be accomplished easily by the re-arrangement of items in the classrooms and hallways. Place books and supplies in an orderly fashion, and, where possible, install cabinets or doors on shelves so that the cluttered areas are covered up and a smooth surface results. Most schools hang pictures, completed assignments, and other projects that the children create on the walls and in the hallways. Get rid of this visual clutter. Why not limit those displays to specific areas within the school, such as a "Hall of Accomplishment" or a "Wall of Dreams"? Take the children on regular tours to the designated hallway or wall. That way, rather than becoming inured to the work of others, they can also share in their creations with an appropriate attitude. Why not make those accomplishments special? They are! As an alternative to aural overload, background music of a nonrepetitive nature can help create an atmosphere that is at once calm and balanced. It can also cover up smaller interruptions in sound.

Color is also extremely important when creating a peaceful, less chaotic environment that is conducive to learning. Unfortunately, most schools go with institutional gray or green. As I have said before, color is energy—it actually has frequency, and these frequencies can affect our moods and even our performance. To create a positive environment, bright, light colors are a must. Combinations of these colors within a single room can change the way that room looks and feels. Pastels such as light yellow, purple, violet, blue, rose, pink, and green (sage or grass green also work) are all good choices. Earth tones tend to create too much of a grounded feeling in a classroom setting, so stay away from those—unless the intent is for the children to take long naps! Also, stay away from dark, intense colors such as deep blues or reds.

ARRANGING THE ROOM

Once the appropriate color atmosphere is created, there are other things that can make a positive difference as well. First, alleviate sharp corners and angles whenever possible in the arrangement and type of furniture. The optimal classroom would be round with no corners at all. This would create a softer environment more in line with sacred geometry—the shapes that are the building blocks of creation. Arrange things in the room geometrically so that there is neatness and order. Within all of us there is an innate recognition of geometric form, and these forms can have interesting and positive effects on everyone. The shapes that are particularly beneficial are a few of those found in what are called the "platonic solids." These consist of the most basic shapes in creation: the sphere, the four-sided pyramid, the cube, and the square. These shapes are appealing to the eye and conducive to learning.

As stated previously, classrooms are generally arranged in regimented rows of seats or tables. Instead, break up the regimented feeling and make the setting more personal. Separate the desks or tables into smaller groups of children who are similarly skilled. If the class isn't too large, create one big circle. Take superiority and the insinuation of comparison out of the equation. Make the teachers a part of the group by putting them in the circle, or in the center of it. The message that is created by this arrangement is that everyone is equally important. In addition, the children are able to see each other, they can interact more easily, and no one is distracted by having someone in front of them or behind them. The setting instantly becomes more intimate and personal. The circular arrangement also makes it easier to place children in groups of similar achievement, or mix the children so that their skills actually complement each other. In this type of situation the children learn to work together, challenge each other, and grow as a team. They gain pride in their interactions and develop life skills such as loyalty, friendship, responsibility, and communication.

For the compartmental thinker, a circular format has other benefits as well. An assignment or a problem question could be introduced into the middle of the group table. The children could be instructed that their circle is like the face of a clock. The question in the middle is where the hands of the cock are fastened. Each child, sitting at a different position around the table, contributes his or her perspective on the question. In other words, the child at the 12 o'clock position would begin, stating his or her opinion and insight about the issue at hand. The next child at, say, 2 o'clock, would have to find another perspective from which to look at the issue. And so it would go around the table. Then discussion amongst the children would ultimately bring forward a well-considered solution.

NATURAL TOUCHES

The Children of Now are extremely aware of their environment, nature, and the planet in general. Live plants contribute greatly to a more natural setting. Other living things are simple yet powerful additions to the classroom— a large aquarium of fish, small animals that can be nurtured and studied by the children, and even visiting pets on special occasions will all create a living and peaceful atmosphere for the teacher and the students. Running water in the form of a small fountain cleanses the energy within the room, and adds natural background sound that will soften the harshness of the surroundings.

Another great way to encourage calm and positive attitude is to take the classes outside when the weather permits. Allow the kids to bring a mat or blanket that will function as their outside space. Allow them to take off their shoes (if they are old enough to put them back on later) and feel the grass under their feet. Encourage them to close their eyes and feel the breeze, and after they have relaxed for a few minutes, have them sit in their personal space and participate in the lessons at hand. Movement such as t'ai chi, stretching, or the occasional free-form dance livens up the children's attention and energy level. This can be done either first thing in the morning, or just after lunch to work off the inevitable after-meal sleepiness. School can be fun with little effort!

LESS STRUCTURE, MORE COMFORT

Often the school day is filled with rigid structure, which includes certain classes at certain times, and deadlines for accomplishment and completion of assignments—all of which create an inordinate pressure on many children to perform. Because the New Kids think compartmentally, they are quite capable of multitasking throughout the day. Instead of working in a linear format, it would be more beneficial to create a wheel system where there are perhaps five or so activities or groups of activities that are progressive. On a set day, assignments are given in various subjects, and the material for each subject is located at a kiosk in a specific area. Each subject stands alone with papers to be done, books to be read, stories to be interpreted, and so on—all available at the kiosk particular to that subject. Ground rules must be set, but the order of accomplishment of assignments is left to the child. He or she may work on more than one subject or assignment at once, but cannot progress to the next step on the wheel until each task on the assigned level of the wheel is completed. The point is that the children don't do a week's worth of math in a day and nothing else. They have levels of achievement they must complete, yet they are given choices in the matter so that they can work at a comfortable pace.

School systems that implement the wheel scheme immediately discover that many of the children who once appeared to be ADD or ADHD will begin to excel. The children have the opportunity to work ahead if they finish their level of the day or week, and those who are a bit slower are not as pressured to compete with others. Competition can be an excellent learning tool as long as it is done responsibly and with integrity. Overt comparison of children, however, is not good at any time. Each child is different, and each has a particular perspective and opinion about any given situation. Comparing children to each other can cause them to question or doubt their validity, which in turn can lead to issues of self-worth.

WELCOME OPEN COMMUNICATION

Communication is one of the greatest assets we can offer to our special children. Most of the time in school they are told what to do and when to do it, but rarely how or why all of that is going to happen. They are not told what will happen later, so they have no idea of what to expect. A child who knows what is coming feels much more secure in his or her experience than a child who does not. Often, the unknown creates stress, but this can easily be avoided through clear and consistent communication.

In every classroom there are times when certain children will become disruptive. Issues come up in class or on the playground, and generally someone is punished or reprimanded and life goes on. However, for the children who witnessed the events or were part of it, those issues often remain unresolved. Recently I was delighted to hear of a private school that sets aside time each day for open discussion among the children. That time in their circle is considered a "safe zone" where the children can state their feelings openly to the teacher and to each other without fear of judgment or repercussion. The children are allowed to say what is in their hearts and on their minds, to express concerns, and even tell other children how they feel about their experiences with them in the classroom. Of course, this forum is supervised and encouraged by the staff, and necessarily has some boundary rules to keep the conversations in a positive and constructive light. What the administrators of the school are finding as they allow this wonderful process is that the children are much more comfortable and at ease, and much more communicative in general.

Many children who act out do so because they are seeking attention, arc simply bored, or have other issues that are not being discussed or resolved either at school or at home. In a more positive setting, disruptive children can learn that their actions are not acceptable to the other children. But they also hear good things about themselves (this is part of the rules), so that, instead of getting negative reinforcement for their actions, they learn from the acceptance of caring people that their behavior can change easily and yield a positive outcome, without a fight or struggle.

Generally speaking, supporting the Children of Now simply requires good common sense, the willingness to make the effort, and consistency all the way around. If we can have the foresight to give our children what they need at home, in their schools, and in social situations, we will raise an amazing generation of sensitive, gifted people who can and will take our world to unbelievable heights of coalescence and accomplishment, for the highest and best experience of the collective.

So What's Next?

Chapter 14

With all of these changes and fast-forward evolution, where do we go from here? What will happen next? First, if we are not resistant to the inevitable transformation of the human race, and we learn to embrace the changes and allow them to blossom out of the infinite possibilities that all of creation has to offer, we will gradually find our world becoming a place that is filled with remarkable promise. We will experience a spontaneous awakening of our giftedness on infinite levels. As some of us respond to these changes with ease, others will too. The consciousness of all people can and will rise to a greater, more positive experience if we have the courage to consciously and intentionally participate in our evolution and empower our children and ourselves toward positive change.

The Crystalline energy fields of the Children of Now have already begun to lighten. They will fade into a rainbow of pastel colors, and eventually into a pure white light. As those changes occur, the evolutionary process will gain momentum. Soon we will witness the dawn of a different kind of humanity, one that remembers its roots, its Source. Humanity will be one that is borne of endless history and infinite future. We will experience new and exciting ways of perceiving reality, and recognize the oneness within ourselves, within others, and within all things.

As time marches forward, more and more of the Children of Now will step into responsible positions as leaders who will change the world socially, politically, and technologically. Their lessons of greatness will include embracing perfection and unconditional inclusion, to the full benefit of everyone. Soon, in about 12 years, there will be another wave of children born of the Earth and beyond. Many of them will come into our world fully realized, carrying memories of infinite time, from before our known history to far into the future. They will apply all of those memories and vast knowledge to everyone they touch and every place that they grace with their presence.

The New Children will bring gifts to our world that we cannot even begin to fathom at this time. They will be children of the white light, carrying every frequency with harmonic perfection in a fully balanced spectrum of light that comes from the Source of all things. These children's energy fields will spiral, constantly reinventing themselves in every moment. They will be gifted telepaths, empaths, healers, teachers, and spiritual leaders—even before they can speak. Their mere presence will forever change the lives of those around them. The children of the white light will completely embrace their gifts, using them instinctively and without hesitation. They will be magical creatures—wise ones who step out of vast reality and into our world as Masters of all time. They will bring examples of greater existence for us to see, and will demonstrate what has always been and what can be in our world again—if we will only open our hearts and remember that *we are one and love is all there is.*

Above all, we must continue to consider the Children of Now. As our evolution continues through our children, we must act to change our environments, schools, homes, and relationships. We must remember to remain flexible; with these kids, anything is possible! The Children of Now are the ones who need us now. As we learn to support them, we support ourselves in the process, and we prepare for the next magical wave of our future generations.

As my friend Nicholas says, we must listen deeply to our children. It isn't too late. Right now is a perfect time to begin.

APPENDIX
MORE INFORMATION ABOUT THE CHILDREN OF NOW

Folowing are lists of Websites, books, and films that offer a great deal of information about the Children of Now. Please bear in mind that these are not recommendations, as the author has not read or seen every item. Most have been recommended to the author by parents, teachers, and professionals who work with the children of Now. These are offered as optional tools for learning about the children. As with all other information available out there, please use your discretion.

INDIGO WEBSITES

✦ *www.indigochild.com*

- *www.artakiane.com/home.htm*
  (The site of Akiane, child prodigy of art and soul.)
- *www.greatdreams.com/indigo.htm*
- *www.indigochild.net/a_homeframe.htm*
  (An international site.)
- *www.childrenofthenewearth.com*
  (The magazine's Website—provides information about raising Indigo and Crystalline Children.)
- *www.indigochildren.meetup.com*
  (Provides information about parent and child groups in your area.)
- *www.experiencefestival.com/indigo_children*
  (Provides links to other resources.)
- *www.starchild.co.za/articles.html*
  (Provides many links to other articles and sites on both Indigo and Crystalline Children.)

CRYSTALLINE WEBSITES

- *www.spiritlite.com*
  (Author's Website.)
- *www.childrenofthenewearth.com*
- *www.nicholas.citymax.com/indigo_nicholas.*
  (Nicholas's Website.)
- *www.thecrystalchildren.com*
- *web.mac.com/LorrinsWorld*
  (Lorrin's Website.)
- *www.lightworker.com/beacons/101502Awakening CrystalChildren*
  (Provides channelings from Steve Rother; these appear in the *Sedona Journal of Emergence* as well.)

✦ *www.metagifted.org/topics/metagifted/crystal Children*
(A general information site with links to many others.)

✦ *www.experiencefestival.com/Crystal_Children*
(Provides many links to other resources.)

✦ *www.enchantedlearning.com/Home*

✦ *www.learnnc.org/index.nsf*

✦ *www.ket.org/cgi-plex/watchseries.pl?&id =AJONO*

✦ *www.learner.org/jnorth*

✦ *www.childrenofthenewearth.com/infoforteachers/ index*

✦ *www.theindigoevolution.com*

✦ *www.cosmikids.org*

✦ *www.childrenlights.com*

✦ *www.planetlightworker.com*

For Further Reading

✦ *Attention-Deficit Disorder: Natural Alternatives to Drug Therapy* (Natural Health Guide) by Nancy L. Morse.

✦ *ADD: The Natural Approach* by Nina Anderson and Howard Peiper (also available on audio cassette).

✦ *Without Ritalin: A Natural Approach to ADD* by Samuel A. Berne.

✦ *Natural Treatments for ADD and Hyperactivity* by Skye Weintraub.

- *Bach Flower Remedies for Children: A Parents' Guide* by Barbara Mazzarella.
- *The Essential Flower Essence Handbook* by Lila Devi.
  (Shows how to use flower essences to assist in emotional balance and support of children and teens.)
- *Beyond the Indigo Children: The New Children and the Coming of the Fifth World* by P.M.H. Atwater.
- *Indigo Children* by Lee Carroll and Jan Tober.
- *Indigo Celebration* by Lee Carroll.
- *Creative Activities for Young Children* by Mary Mayesky.
- *The Secret Spiritual World of Children* by Tobin Hart, Ph.D.
- *Raising Your Spirited Child: A Guide for Parents Whose Child is More Intense, Sensitive, Perceptive, Persistent, and Energetic* by Mary Sheedy Kurcinka.
- *Raising Psychic Children: Messages from "Thomas"* by James F. Twyman.
- *Emissary of Love* by James Twyman.
  (Visit his Website at *www.emissaryoflight.com*, or e-mail him at james@emissarybooks.com.)

KIDS BOOKS

- *Full Moon Stories—Thirteen Native American Legends by Eagle Walking Turtle Arrow: A Pueblo Indian Tale* by Gerald McDermott.

+ *Places of Power* by Michael DeMunn.
(Teaches of sanctity of sacred places and children's own holiness.)

+ *Native Plant Stories* by Joseph Bruchac.
(Teaches "listening to plants" and receiving their "medicine.")

+ *The Sacred Tree* by Four Worlds Development Project.
(Teaches the gifts of the Four Directions).

+ *The Little Soul and the Sun,* by Neale Donald Walsh
(Teaches children about their true soul origin.)

+ *SunDancer Speaks of Life, Death and Freedom: We are the Generators of the Myths, Stories and Legends of a Future Age* by Edward Hays.

+ *Hope for the Flowers: A Tale Partly About Life, Partly About Revolution and Lots of Hope for Adults and Others (Including Caterpillars Who Can Read)* by Trina Paulus.

+ *Special Gifts: In Search of Love and Honor* by Dennis L. Olson.
(A charming tale of the Creator seeking advice from the animals.)

+ *The Children's Book of Virtues* by William J. Bennett.

+ *Children of The Sun: A Spiritual Journey Using Story and Songs* by Laurel Savoie and Emery Bear (includes CD).

FILM

✦ *The Indigo Evolution*, by James Twyman, Stephen Simon, Kent Romney, and Doreen Virtue.

OTHER VALUABLE LINKS

✦ *www.healingarts.org/children/holmes.htm#exam* (Site of Amy S. Holmes, M.D. Offers options for the treatment of autism.)

✦ *www.cem.msu.edu/~cem181h/projects/97/mercury/ #anchor233568* (Site of Andrew Volz, Jake Weaver, and Dean Shooltz. Discusses mercury toxicity in the human brain.)

✦ *www.academy.d20.co.edu/kadets/lundberg/dna* (Shows pictures of human DNA.)

✦ *articles.news.aol.com/news/article* (Offers more information about DNA nutrition.)

✦ *www.drboylan.com* (Site of Richard Boylan; see also the 42 signs that a child is a Star Child at *www.drboylan.com/strkidsigns*.)

INDEX

aspects as harmonized set of
frequencies, 138
aspects, definition of, 135
attention deficit disorder, *see*
ADD
attention deficit/hyperactivity
disorder, *see* ADHD
aural and visual inputs as
factors in Children of
Now's comfort, 205
autism, 51-54
mercury toxicity and, 53
sense of touch and, 52-53
awareness, creating, 197

B

Beautiful Silent Ones
and telepathic
communication 147-149
as deceiving to our
senses, 167
Beautiful Silent Ones, parallel
aspects and the, 144
bodies, Children of Now
listening to their, 211-212
brain waves and new
patterns, 50
Brian, 158-167
bridge to higher
consciousness,
Children of Now as, 31
Brittany, 176-178

C

categories of children, 21-22
checklist for recognizing
Crystalline Children, 107
Chief Golden Eagle, 160, 161
Children of Now
and evolutionary change, 32
and new energy systems, 44
and universal
communication
system, 44
as bridge to higher
consciousness, 31
communicating in our
world, 41
Children of Now
classification of, 25
gifts of, 30
stories of, 26
Children of the Stars
description of, 111
classroom
arrangement of the,
226-228
color in the, 226
communication in,
230-231
living things as part
of, 228
visual clutter in the, 225
classroom circumstances and
Crystallines, 99
collective consciousness as
emotionally based, 78

ABOUT THE AUTHOR

Meg Blackburn Losey, Ph.D., is also the author of *Pyramids of Light: Awakening to Multi-Dimensional Reality* and *The Online Messages*. She has recently worked as a consultant to *Good Morning America*, and is the hostess of *The Dr. Meg Show: Conscious Talk for Greater Reality*. Dr. Meg is the developer of Movement to Spirit and the Seventh Sense Attunement healing technique. She resides in the mountains of Tennessee. Dr. Meg can be reached through her Website at *www.spiritlite.com*, or via e-mail at drmeg@spiritlite.com.

Also Available from New Page Books:

Conversation With the Children of Now
Meg Blackburn Losey
Foreword by Lee Carroll
EAN 978-1-56414-978-7

"Meg Blackburn is at the forefront of the exposure of these kids, with the core resources... the kids themselves. With permission from their parents, she has given you a book that lets you wander into their minds and see what they are thinking, and in the process lets you decide for yourself if the children of this planet are changing."
—Lee Carroll, author of *Indigo Children*

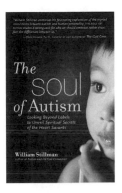

The Soul of Autism
Looking Beyond Labels to Unveil Spiritual Secrets of the Heart Savants
William Stillman
EAN 978-1-60163-005-6

"*The Soul of Autism* reveals the often unrecognized spiritual gifts of those 'on the spectrum' and explains how they can help all of us. William Stillman believes the world needs autism. After reading this moving and inspiring book, you will see why."
—Melissa Chianta, managing editor, *Mothering* magazine

"I believe the world owes William Stillman a debt of gratitude for the courage it took him to research and write this book. It is filled with rare wisdom and amazing stories that will totally surprise you!"
—P.M.H. Atwater, author of *Beyond the Indigo Children*

Visit NewPageBooks.com for more information or to download our newest catalog as a PDF.